SUPERGRAINS

seeds, pulses, legumes & nuts

SUPERGRAINS

seeds, pulses, legumes & nuts

VICTORIA MERRETT

CHARTWELL
BOOKS

This edition published in 2015 by
CHARTWELL BOOKS
an imprint of Book Sales
a division of Quarto Publishing Group
USA Inc.
142 West 36th Street, 4th Floor
New York, NY 10018
USA

Copyright © 2015
Regency House Publishing Limited
The Manor House
High Street
Buntingford
Hertfordshire
SG9 9AB
United Kingdom

For all editorial enquiries, please contact:
www.regencyhousepublishing.com

ISBN-13: 978-0-7858-3216-4

Printed in China

This is a beginner's introduction to a
fascinating look into the health benefits
of 'Supergrains.' It does not, however
encourage self-diagnosis and self-
medication and is not an alternative to
orthodox medical advice and treatment.
The author and the publisher cannot
accept any legal responsibility for any
omissions and errors in this book.

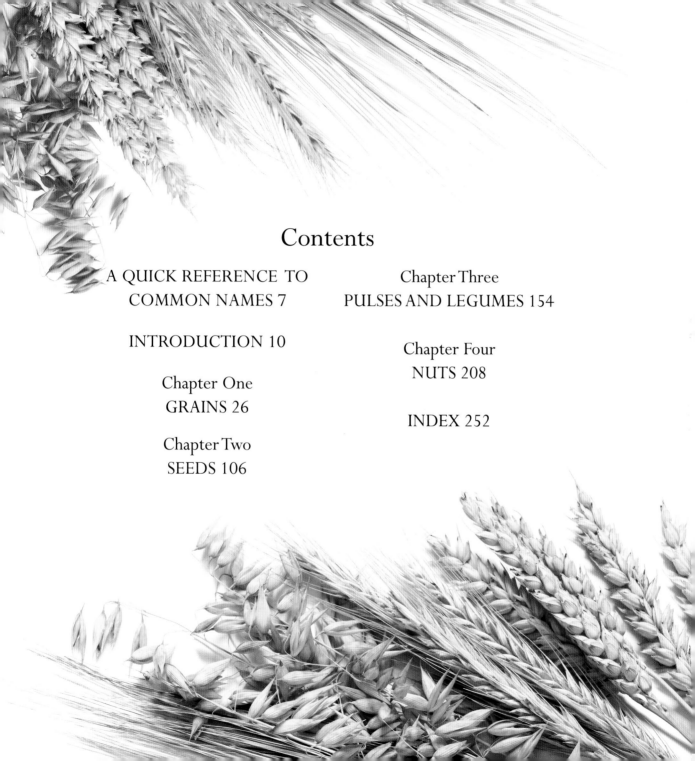

Contents

A QUICK REFERENCE TO COMMON NAMES

INTRODUCTION

The world's most important seed food source, by weight, is cereals, followed by legumes and nuts.

A cereal is a member of the grass family, *Poaceae*, cultivated for the edible components of its grain, and consists of endosperm, germ and bran. Cereal grains are grown in greater quantities and provide more food energy worldwide than any other crop.

A legume is a plant in the family *Fabaceae* (or *Leguminosae*), or the fruit or seed of such a plant. They are grown primarily for their food grain seed (e.g., beans and lentils–known generally as pulses), and as soil-enhancing green manure.

(Legumes are notable in that most of them have symbiotic nitrogen-fixing bacteria in their root nodules.) Legumes are among the best protein sources in the plant kingdom and, being relatively cheap compared with meat, make a good alternative to it in vegetarian and vegan diets.

Nuts are a particular kind of seed, with chestnuts and

OPPOSITE LEFT: Rice grains in their natural state.

OPPOSITE RIGHT: Spelt is widely believed to be the first species of wheat used in the making of bread.

ABOVE: Once considered to be a grain suitable only for animal feed, millet is now gaining popularity as a health food.

RIGHT: A field of wheat.

hazelnuts coming under this definition. In culinary terms, however, it is used more broadly to include fruits that are not botanically qualified as nuts but have a similar appearance, and which include almonds, coconuts and cashew nuts.

Like the whole grains, seeds, legumes and nuts are truly wonderful foods that have been cultivated and consumed for thousands of years. They are high in fiber, full of nutrients and rich in healthy fats. For vegans and vegetarians in particular, seeds and nuts are not only a source of valuable protein, but also of omega fatty acids which are essential for body and brain.

Vegans often rely solely on vegetables and grains as the mainstay of their diet, inevitably missing out on fats, which should

Rice is grown in flooded fields called paddies. In some developing countries the rice is cut by hand with a knife or scythe and will then be threshed in a machine to release the outer hulls.

not be demonized; in fact it would be a mistake to cut back on nuts and oils as a way of minimizing unhealthy fats. Perfect for filling this nutritional gap, especially for those completely eschewing meat and dairy products, is a daily portion of seeds, legumes and/or nuts. Remember that a mere ounce a day is enough to provide the immunity-boosting nutrients that the body needs.

We have been eating cereal grains for thousands of years and some of them, such as barley, emmer (farro) and freekeh, are among the most ancient, dating back as far as 9000 BC to the Fertile Crescent in the Middle East, where they were first cultivated. Other grains were also known in antiquity, including millet and spelt, while rice may have been grown in what is now Thailand since 4000 BC.

The first cultivated grains were subjected to some degree of processing to make them edible, although early processing was

probably negligible and most were eaten in very nearly their raw state. It is likely, however, that the early cereals were cooked, once this became possible, to make them more palatable after the indigestible outer hulls had been removed. Eventually, the milling process was established, which produced flour which was relatively easy to handle and store.

Along with hulling and milling, it was also discovered that grains could be preserved, with sun-drying being one of the oldest methods. Drying removes moisture from the food stuff and

OPPOSITE: Legumes include peas, beans, lentils, peanuts, etc. All are inexpensive nutrient-rich sources of protein.

RIGHT: Quinoa has recently come to be considered a 'supergrain' due to its high nutritional content. The seeds are cooked in much the same way as rice and used in a wide range of dishes.

prevents spoilage – a method that has also been used for preserving certain vegetables, fruits, meats, fish, etc.

In time, the storage and processing of grains was perfected, which meant that larger-scale civilizations could flourish, nomadic lifestyles diminish, and more settled ways of life adopted, encouraging further population growth. Trading with other cultures began to develop in earnest once farmers began to produce surplus crops.

European explorers brought wheat to the Americas, and colonists in New England first grew the plant in 1602. It did not become an important crop until settlers began to filter west to the prairies, where the land and the climate was more suitable. Eventually, that area came to be known as the country's 'bread

basket,' making the United States a world exporter of wheat.

Most of us already know that fruits and vegetables contain beneficial phytochemicals and antioxidants conducive to good health, although grains, seeds and legumes have been somewhat overlooked as potential health-giving 'superfoods.' So much so, that in relatively recent times, carbohydrate-rich foods have come to be seen in a negative light, having been linked with unwanted weight-gain, gluten sensitivity and allergies. What seems to have been forgotten is that these foods, particularly when consumed in their wholegrain form, are fiber-rich,

supply necessary glucose to the body and brain, and are loaded with vitamins, minerals, antioxidants and other important nutrients not always present in fruits and vegetables.

There will always be exceptions to the rule, and it must be

OPPOSITE & RIGHT: Whole grains are an essential part of a healthy diet, being good sources of complex carbohydrates and various key vitamins and minerals.

Beans (also known as legumes or pulses) belong to an extremely large category of vegetables containing more than 13,000 species and are second only to grains in supplying calories and protein to the world's population.

remembered that people with celiac disease cannot tolerate gluten, a protein in wheat, rye and barley which causes the body to react by attacking the intestinal villi responsible for absorbing nutrients, leaving the sufferer susceptible to malnutrition.

All is not lost, however, and there are plenty of other grains which do not contain gluten or other allergens or are very low in them. Gluten-free grains include buckwheat, proso millet, quinoa and rice, while seeds and legumes are also gluten-free. Oats also come into this category, but may possibly become tainted with other gluten-containing foods during processing.

Whole grains contain all the nutrients that occur naturally in the grain. When processed, these are removed, resulting in white bread, for example. Some wheat breads are 'enriched,' whereby, supposedly, some of the nutrients are 'put back.' Once the nutrients are removed, however, their biochemical structure and associated nutrients and fiber are irrevocably destroyed.

It follows, therefore, that whole grains are by far the best choice. Grains are considered to be whole when all three parts, i.e., the bran, germ and endosperm, have been left intact and in their original proportions. Often, the most beneficial nutrients lie in the outer parts of the grain which are stripped away during processing. Unprocessed plain grains should form a regular part of your daily diet, while processed grains should be taken in moderation.

A diet rich in whole grains has been shown to reduce the risk of heart attack, heart disease in general, type 2 diabetes, obesity and some forms of cancer. This will also ensure healthy bowel function and improve the regularity of bowel movements.

OPPOSITE: Home-made muesli is great for breakfast or as a grab-and-go snack. It can be customized with the grains, seeds and dried fruits of your choice.

Eating more whole grain foods provides a reduced risk of asthma, inflammatory disease, colorectal cancer and gum disease. It has also been shown to have a beneficial effect on the carotid arteries and helps to maintain a healthy blood pressure.

Shopping for whole grain products can often be overwhelming in that descriptions tend to be misleading. Terms like multi-grain, brown, organic or stoneground do not always indicate a healthier product and it is important to read the labeling carefully before buying them.

Historically, many cultures developed food preparation and cooking techniques, such as soaking, sprouting, roasting and fermentation, which made whole grains, legumes, nuts and seeds easier to digest and their nutrients more bio-available. Beans,

for example, were soaked overnight before cooking and wheat was slow fermented before baking. Traditionally, nuts and seeds have also been gently dry-

roasted to make them easier to digest and release their flavorsome oils.

In the main, traditional cultures have tended to use whole grains but, in some, refined grains, such as polished rice, continue to be used. Traditional Chinese and Indian cultures choose polished rice over brown, which may be easier to digest but is lacking in valuable components. To some extent, however, this is compensated for by their use of healthy amounts of pulses and vegetables and good cooking practice. In Western cuisine, polished rice is often seen as a replacement for potatoes.

There are various ways of preparing grains, seeds, nuts and legumes for eating. In their dried form some need more soaking or prolonged cooking than others to soften them or remove dangerous toxins. It is therefore essential that all suppliers' instructions are followed to the letter to avoid possible poisoning.

CAUTION:

INTOLERANCES & ALLERGIES

Most grains, seeds and nuts are safe to eat, but certain people have intolerances, allergies or have been prescribed certain medications that may trigger adverse reactions. It is essential, therefore, that medical advice is sought in these rare cases.

It must be stressed that it is the healthiest option to adopt a balanced diet, composed of all food types, rather than concentrate on a restricted one which may lead to nutritional imbalance and even, unusually, produce toxic effects.

Food intolerances and allergies, which affect nearly everyone at some time or another, are detrimental reactions to a food, beverage or additive which can be delayed or occur immediately after exposure. There is a difference, however, between a true food allergy or hypersensitivity, which is an abnormal response to a food

Sunflower seeds are particularly rich in Vitamin E, an antioxidant which is important in the prevention of heart disease.

triggered by the immune system. A food intolerance, however, is not triggered by the immune system but can seem like an allergy.

People with true food allergies must identify the offending foods and avoid them or seek advice from a qualified medical practitioner, remembering that reactions can be devastating or even fatal.

There are a wide range of symptoms which occur when the body has an intolerance. These may include fatigue, weight gain, bloating, nausea, diarrea, digestive complaints, rashes, joint pain, yeast infections, urinary tract infections or iron deficiencies. For this reason it is essential that any known food items, which may cause such effects, be avoided completely and medical advice sought.

GRAINS

CHAPTER ONE

GRAINS

AMARANTH

Botanical name: *Amaranthus tricolor*
Family: *Amaranthaceae*

Amaranth has been cultivated as a grain for 8,000 years. It was a staple food, along with corn and beans, of the Aztecs, Incas and Mayans and was an integral part of their culture, used in religious ceremonies. The Aztecs referred to amaranth as the 'golden grain of the gods,' while other pre-Columbian peoples believed it to have supernatural powers. It was their custom to mix amaranth flour with human blood and form the dough into shapes representing their idols, which they would then use in sacrificial rites and ceremonies.

In the 1500s the Spanish conquistadors tried to ban the consumption of amaranth in an attempt to gain control over the Aztecs, but their efforts were fruitless, in that amaranth grows like a weed requiring little cultivation, which makes it virtually impossible to eradicate. Consequently, it flourished in the more inaccessible parts of Central and South America and its gene pool was thus preserved. Different species of amaranth spread throughout the world during the 17th, 18th and 19th centuries, and its use became widespread in Himalayan regions and elsewhere.

Amaranth seed flour is used to make bread, pastas and polenta, while the seeds can be used whole and added to breakfast cereals, soups, muesli bars, cookies, etc. Amaranth grain is an especially good source of plant protein in that it contains two essential amino acids, lysine and methionine, making it of value to

Health benefits: Amaranth grain is thought to improve hair quality, making hair loss and graying less likely. It can lower (bad) cholesterol and reduce the risk of cardiovascular disease. It is full of antioxidants and particularly high in vitamin C which is unusual for a grain. It is also loaded with many other important vitamins and minerals. Amaranth is good for the eyesight and is an appetite suppressant for those trying to lose weight.

Amaranth grains (left) and popped amaranth (below).

vegans and vegetarians. It is also rich in iron, magnesium and calcium and high in fiber while, being completely gluten-free and easily digestible, it is an ideal wheat substitute for those on a gluten-free diet.

In Mexico it is popped and mixed with sugar, while in Peru it is used to make beer. Amaranth has a unique, sweet, earthy, nutty flavor. Since the 1970s it has been gaining popularity throughout the world since its properties have been rediscovered; it can be found in health food stores.

AMARANTH BANANA BREAD

1¼ cups whole wheat pastry flour
¾ cup amaranth flour
2 tsp baking powder
½ tsp baking soda
½ tsp salt
3 very ripe bananas
1 tsp vanilla extract
2 large eggs
⅓ cup fat-free plain yogurt
2 tbsp canola oil, plus more for
 oiling the pan
¾ cup sugar
1 cup walnuts, roughly chopped

Serves 6–8

1 Preheat the oven to 350°F.
Lightly oil a 9 x 5-inch loaf pan.

2 In a large bowl, whisk together
the whole wheat pastry flour,
amaranth flour, baking powder,
baking soda and salt. In a separate
bowl, whisk together the bananas,
vanilla extract, eggs, yogurt, oil
and sugar. Add the banana
mixture to the flour mixture and
stir until just combined. Fold in
half the walnuts. Pour the batter
into the prepared pan and top
with the remaining walnuts.

3 Bake for 1 hour or until the
bread is golden brown and a
skewer inserted in the center of
the loaf comes out clean. Leave to
cool slightly, then loosen the sides
from the pan. Remove the loaf and
serve warm. Alternatively, leave to
cool completely before serving.

AMARANTH PANCAKES

2 eggs
½ cup milk
2 tsp coconut oil
½ cup amaranth flour
½ cup tapioca flour
6 tsp arrowroot
½ tsp cinnamon
½ tsp baking powder
¼ tsp salt

Serves 2–4

1 Beat the eggs, then add the milk and oil and beat again.

2 In a separate bowl, mix all the dry ingredients together. Add the dry ingredients to the egg mixture, a little at a time, mixing well after each addition.

3 Spray a griddle or skillet with cooking oil. Drop large spoonfuls of the batter onto the griddle, being careful not to overcrowd them, and cook until bubbles form on the surfaces and the edges become dry. (This will take 3–4 minutes.) Flip and cook on the other sides for 2–3 minutes until lightly browned. Repeat until all the batter is used up.

OAT

Botanical name: *Avena sativa*
Family: *Poaceae*

The common oat is a cereal grain that has evolved from its wild ancester in the Near East. The domesticated oat dates back to the Bronze Age in Europe, and today

is grown in all temperate regions of the world, being more tolerant of colder, wetter weather and poorer soil conditions than other cereals; it can even be grown as far north as Iceland.

Oats are a constituent of numerous foods and are widely used in animal feeds. Commonly fed to horses in hard work, such as racehorses, oats provide the extra energy to allow the animal compete. Oat straw is very often used as animal bedding due to its soft texture.

Oats can be milled into flour or crushed or bruised and added to breakfast cereals, cakes, cookies and mueslis. In Britain, they are used in the brewing of a kind of beer known as stout.

High in carbohydrates and supplying slow-release energy, oats also provide many other important nutrients and fiber which are vital for good health. Today, oats are regarded as a health food, which is a far cry from the days when they were the staple diet of the Scots, who had difficulties growing some of the other, less hardy cereals.

One of the more traditional ways to cook with oats, is to start the day with a piping-hot bowl of oatmeal porridge, to which fruits and nuts may be added. Oats can also be used in cookie recipes, breads and muffins to make them more texturally interesting and nutritious.

HEALTH BENEFITS: Although oats are usually hulled, this process does not strip away all the nutrients. Oats are known for lowering (bad) cholesterol which in turn reduces the risk of cardiovascular disease, and they are of particular benefit to postmenopausal women. The beneficial components in oats help to ward off infections, stabilize blood sugars, moderate childhood asthma and even protect against some cancers.

ENGLISH FLAPJACKS

½ cup butter
½ packed cup brown sugar
4 tbs corn or golden syrup
3 cups rolled oats
¼ cup dried cranberries

Serves 6–8

1 Preheat the oven to 350°F.

2 In a pan set over a low heat, combine the butter, brown sugar and syrup, stirring occasionally until the butter and sugar have completely melted. Stir in the oats, then add the cranberries, coating them well. Pour into a 7- or 8-inch square baking pan. (The mixture should be about 1 inch thick.)

3 Bake for 30 minutes until the top is golden. Cut the flapjacks into squares, then leave to cool completely before removing them from the pan.

OATMEAL & RAISIN COOKIES

¾ cup soft butter

¾ cup white sugar

¾ packed cup light brown sugar

2 eggs

1 tsp vanilla extract

1¼ cups all-purpose flour

1 tsp baking soda

¾ tsp ground cinnamon

½ tsp salt

2¾ cups rolled oats

1 cup raisins

Serves 6–8

1 Preheat the oven to 375°F.

2 In a large bowl, cream together the butter and white and brown sugars until smooth.

3 Beat in the eggs and vanilla extract until the mixture is fluffy.

4 In another bowl, stir together the flour, baking soda, cinnamon and salt, then gradually beat into the butter mixture. Stir in the oats and raisins. Using a spoon, drop teaspoonfuls of the mixture onto an ungreased cookie sheet, leaving space for the mixture to spread.

5 Bake for 8–10 minutes or until golden brown, then allow to cool slightly before transferring to a wire rack. Cool completely before eating.

QUINOA
Botanical name: *Chenopodium quinoa*
Family: *Chenopodiaceae*

Quinoa, known for its starchy, edible seeds, is a species of goosefoot and is related to beet, spinach and tumbleweed. It is not a true cereal but is known instead as a pseudocereal because it is not a member of the grass family.

Quinoa, pronounced 'kinwa,' was first seen in the Andes where it was domesticated 3,000 to 4,000 years ago and in pre-Columbian times was an important part of the Andean diet. The grain-like seeds were eaten in Bolivia, Peru and Colombia where they were a diet staple. The Incas called quinoa 'the mother of all grains,' so much did they value its importance. During the Spanish conquest, however, the colonists scorned it as 'food for Indians,' and suppressed its cultivation due to its importance in native religious ceremonies; but they were unable to eradicate the plant completely.

During the last ten years, quinoa has come to be regarded as a 'supergrain' due to its nutritive

commercially, however, has fortunately been processed to remove this bitter coating.

Quinoa can be prepared for eating in much the same way as most other grains, which can be simmered in water or in a rice cooker or added to pilafs, casseroles and soups. Cooked quinoa is light and fluffy in texture with a nutty, slightly chewy texture.

Heath benefits: Quinoa is recommended for a number of conditions, being of benefit to migraine sufferers and to those with heart disease and atherosclerosis, as well as for celiacs. It is considered to be a healthy choice for all striving to achieve a balanced diet or for those trying to lose weight. Its lysine and other amino acid content makes it of particular benefit to vegans and vegetarians.

LEFT: Cooked quinoa.

BELOW: White and red quinoa grains.

qualities and the fact that it is very high in protein for a pseudocereal. It is a good source of dietary fiber, phosphorus, magnesium, iron and calcium and, being gluten-free, is easy to digest.

Quinoa grains have a unique outer coating called saponin, which affords them a natural protection from the sun's rays and from birds, in that it causes the grain to taste quite bitter and unpalatable in its natural state. Much of the grain sold

QUINOA SALAD

1 tsp canola oil
1 tsp minced garlic
2½ cups water
2 tsp salt
¼ tsp ground black pepper
2 cups quinoa
½ cup chopped hazelnuts
1 packed cup chopped arugula
1 red bell pepper, deseeded and
 chopped
2 tbsp olive oil
3 tbsp white wine vinegar

Serves 4

1 Heat the oil in a pot over a
medium heat. Add the garlic and
cook until translucent but not
browned. Pour in the water, the
salt and pepper, and bring to a
boil. Stir in the quinoa, then reduce
the heat to medium-low and cover.
Simmer until the quinoa is tender
(about 20 minutes). Drain any
remaining water from the quinoa
and transfer it to a large mixing
bowl. Refrigerate until cold.

2 Stir the hazelnuts, arugula
and bell pepper into the quinoa.
Drizzle with the olive oil and
vinegar and stir until evenly
mixed.

QUINOA PUDDING

1½ cups water
¾ cup quinoa
2 cups whole milk
2 tbsp white sugar
Pinch of salt
½ tbsp butter
½ tsp vanilla extract
1 cup fresh berries

Serves 4

1 Rinse and drain the quinoa. Bring the water and quinoa to a boil in a pot over a high heat, stirring occasionally. Reduce the heat, cover, and simmer for 15 minutes. Remove from the heat.

2 Add the milk, sugar and salt to the pot with the quinoa.

3 Place the pot over a medium heat and cook, stirring, until the mixture becomes thick and creamy (5–10 minutes). Remove from the heat, then stir in the butter and vanilla extract. Can be served warm or cold, garnished with whatever fresh berries you like.

BUCKWHEAT

Botanical name: *Fagopyrum esculentum*
Family: *Polygonaceae*

Buckwheat is also known as beech wheat, but despite its names it is neither related to wheat, nor is it technically a grass; it is more often described as a pseudocereal. It is cultivated for its grain-like seeds, however, and is also used as a cover crop.

Buckwheat is related to sorrel, knotweed and rhubarb. Its flowers are very fragrant, making it attractive to bees which use them to produce a special, strongly-flavored dark honey.

Buckwheat was first domesticated and cultivated some 6,000 years ago in Central Asia and Tibet before spreading throughout the Middle East and Europe and then later to other parts of the world. The plant grows well in acid and poor soils but needs good drainage. Today, it is commercially cultivated worldwide but particularly in Russia, China and Ukraine.

Buckwheat is usually sold roasted or unroasted. Unroasted it

is more subtle in flavor, while roasted buckwheat is stronger and with a nuttier taste.

Buckwheat is often used as an alternative to rice and can also be ground into flour. Being gluten-free, it is often used in recipes for pancakes and the like for those who are wheat-intolerant. It can also be treated like hot breakfast oatmeal porridge and can be added as a thickener to soups and stews. In more recent years, it has also been used as a subsitute for other grains in the making of gluten-free beer.

Health benefits: Buckwheat is of benefit to those affected by high blood pressure and cardiovascular problems in general, and is reputed to be helpful in the prevention and treatment of gallstones, diabetes, asthma and intestinal conditions. It has high levels of phytonutrients, particularly flavonoids, which are thought to reduce (bad) cholesterol and consequently prevent strokes.

Buckwheat flour can be made into buckwheat bread, which smells and tastes delicious when freshly baked.

BUCKWHEAT BREAD

½ tsp baker's yeast
2 heaped tsp soft, dark-brown
 sugar
1 cup lukewarm water
3½ cups buckwheat flour
1 cup porridge oats
¾ cup sunflower seeds
¼ cup flaxseeds
¼ cup sesame seeds
1 tsp fine sea salt
1¾ cups water

Serves 6–8

1 In a large bowl, mix together the yeast, sugar and lukewarm water.

2 Add the rest of the ingredients, mixing well by hand, or use a wooden spoon. (The mixture should feel more sticky than wet, but add a little more water if it feels too dry.) Remove any excess mixture from the sides, so that the dough sits in a rough ball in the center of the bowl.

3 Place a clean towel over the bowl and leave in a warm place for 6–8 hours to prove.

4 Preheat the oven to 375°F. Line a medium-sized bread pan with baking parchment. Then, use your hands to briefly knead the dough sufficiently to release any excess gases which may have formed in the proving.

5 Form the risen dough into a rough loaf-like shape and place in the pan, decorating the top if you like.

6 Bake for one hour or until a skewer, inserted into the center, comes out clean. Cook for a little longer if still wet.

7 Remove from the pan and cool on a wire rack, having first sifted a little flour over the top.

BUCKWHEAT PORRIDGE

2–3 cups whole buckwheat,
 soaked in water overnight
Pinch of salt
3 tbsp sugar
½ cup milk or cream

Serves 3–4

1 Drain and rinse the pre-soaked buckwheat.

2 Add the buckwheat to a pot and cover it with fresh water. Add a pinch of salt and cook until the buckwheat is soft.

3 Mix in the sugar and cook, stirring, for a minute or two more.

4 Remove the buckwheat porridge from the heat and add the fresh milk or cream. Serve warm.

BARLEY
Botanical name: *Hordeum vulgare*
Family: *Poaceae*

Barley, one of the most ancient members of the grass family to be domesticated, is among the most important of our cereal crops. Its exact origin is debatable, but it is thought to have come from Egypt, Ethiopia, the Near East or Tibet.

The ancient Greeks cultivated barley and their diet came to be based mainly on the cereal, especially when it was discovered that athletes gained more energy and strength by eating it. The Romans, too, who learned from the Greeks, recognized the high energy value of barley and used it in food prepared for gladiators.

The classical world ended, and barley soon came to be regarded as a food staple, though one suitable only for the poorer classes or animal fodder.

Currently, barley is seldom used in the making of bread except in Tibet, where the cereal is easy to

barley makes a welcome addition to hot oat breakfast porridge.

Like all grains, barley must be thoroughly rinsed prior to cooking. Pearl or pearled barley should be simmered for about an hour, while hulled barley needs about 90 minutes or so to be fully edible.

Heath benefits: Of benefit to sufferers from asthma, arthritis, skin problems, obesity, anemia, constipation, diabetes, high blood pressure and kidney disease. Barley is rich in a variety of proteins and high in fiber. It is believed to prevent gallstones, some cancers, cardiovascular disease, osteoporosis and is good for the skin and the immune system. Barley contains several vitamins and minerals, including vitamin B3, vitamin B1, selenium, iron, magnesium, zinc, phosphorus and copper.

cultivate in the harsher climate. Today, barley is produced across the world and the United States is one of its leading producers.

Barley has a pleasant, nutty flavor and can be used in a variety of ways, while fermented barley is used in beer-making and in the making of other alcoholic drinks. One of the most popular ways of using barley is as a thickener in soups and stews, particularly satisfying in cold, wintry weather. Barley flour can be added to wheat flour to make breads and muffins, while cracked or flaked

SCOTCH BROTH

2¼ lbs neck of lamb or stewing
 lamb with bone, cut into pieces
3 onions, chopped
3 turnips, chopped
2 carrots, chopped
1 tbsp black peppercorns
8 cups water
½ cup pearl barley
1 carrot, diced
1 stick celery, diced
2 onions, minced
1 leek, chopped
2 turnips, diced
Salt and pepper to taste

Serves 6

1 To make the stock, put the lamb,
3 onions, 3 turnips, 2 carrots and
the peppercorns into the water
in a large pot. Bring to a
boil, reduce the heat and
simmer, covered, for
3 hours. Skim the
surface from time to time
as required.

2 Remove the lamb from the
stock, then the meat from the
bones which can be discarded.
Finely chop the meat, then cover
and refrigerate it. Strain
the stock, discarding the

vegetables and refrigerate
overnight or until the fat has set
on top and can be spooned off.

3 The next day, cover the barley
with water and soak for an hour.

4 Put the reserved stock into a
large pot and gently reheat. Add
the drained barley, extra carrot,
celery, onions, leek and turnips
and season well to taste. Bring to a
boil, reduce the heat, and simmer
for 30 minutes or until the barley
and vegetables are just cooked.
Return the reserved meat to the
pan and simmer for 5 minutes.

BARLEY RISOTTO WITH FAVA BEANS & RED ONION

5 cups vegetable or chicken stock
2 tbsp extra-virgin olive oil
1 small red onion, sliced into
 rings
1 cup pearl barley
½ cup white wine
1 cup fresh or frozen fava (broad)
 beans
½ cup freshly grated Parmesan
 cheese, plus more for serving
2 tbsp softened butter
Salt and freshly ground black
 pepper to taste

Serves 3–4

1 Bring the stock to a simmer in a pot set over a moderately high heat, then reduce the heat to low to keep the stock warm.

2 In a large, deep skillet, heat the olive oil, then add the onion and sauté it over a moderate heat, stirring occasionally, until soft but not browned. Remove the onion and place to one side.

3 Add the barley, stirring for 2 minutes, then add the wine, stirring it until absorbed (about one minute). Add 1 cup of the warm stock and continue stirring until nearly absorbed. Continue adding the stock, ½ cup at a time, until 1 cup of stock is left to be added. Ten minutes before the end of cooking time, add the beans. (The risotto will take about 35 minutes to cook until the barley is *al dente* and suspended in a creamy sauce).

4 To finish, stir in the onion rings, Parmesan cheese and butter and season well. Serve the risotto at once, with extra Parmesan cheese sprinkled over the top.

TIP: If you prefer your risotto wetter and softer, add the reserved stock and continue cooking for a few extra minutes.

RISOTTO RICE

Botanical name: *Oryza sativa*
Family: *Poaceae*

Risotto is a traditional Italian rice dish made from a stubby short-grained, starchy variety of rice specifically grown in Italy.

The technique for making risotto involves stirring small amounts of hot stock or broth into the rice a little at a time, allowing the liquid to become gradually absorbed. While it cooks, the rice releases its starch, giving the risotto a loose, rich and creamy consistency known as *all'onda* (flowing like a wave). Risotto is not only versatile but also easy to prepare, though care must be taken to achieve the correct texture of the dish without overcooking the rice.

Risotto rices are varieties of round to medium short-grain rices that are commonly used in the making of risottos. All have the ability to absorb liquids and also release starch during cooking, making them more sticky than other rice varieties.

There are many different varieties of Italian risotto rice, such as Arborio, Baldo, Carnaroli, Maratelli, Padano, Roma and Vialone Nanoall, of which have slightly different properties. For example, Carnaroli is less likely to become overcooked, while other varieties, such as Roma, give a less creamy result: all can vary greatly in price.

The risotto originated in the north of Italy where it is justly popular, from every Italian home to the most exclusive of gourmet restaurants. It is a creamy rice dish, usually containing butter, wine and onions, with meat, fish or vegetables added to make different versions of the dish.

It is usually eaten as a first course in Italy, but elsewhere often becomes the main dish. The most famous version is *Risotto alla Milanese,* which is a slow-cooked risotto flavored and colored with saffron, often served as an accompaniment to *osso buco,* a slow-cooked veal stew.

Health benefits: The nutritional value of rice in general has made it a dietary staple for much of the global population. It is said to help maintain healthy body weight, support cardiovascular health, lower cholesterol, and help prevent type 2 diabetes. Rice is an important source of complex carbohydrates, which supply energy to the body and fuel for the brain. It provides vitamins that include riboflavin, thiamine and niacin, and also contains iron, vitamin D and calcium. Rice contains eight amino acids which makes it a good source of protein.

ASPARAGUS RISOTTO

1 tbsp olive oil
1 shallot, finely chopped
1 stick celery, finely chopped
1 clove garlic, crushed
¾ cup risotto rice (e.g., Carnaroli
 or Arborio)
½ pint dry white wine
3 cups hot chicken or vegetable
 stock (kept warm over heat in a
 separate pot)
6 asparagus spears, blanched and
 chopped into pieces with the tips
 left whole
1 tbsp unsalted butter
½ cup grated Parmesan cheese
Salt and black pepper

Serves 2

1 Heat the olive oil in a skillet and gently sweat the shallot, celery and garlic until soft but not colored.

2 Add the rice and stir around until thoroughly coated in the oil. Add the wine and simmer until it is fully absorbed into the rice.

3 Add the hot stock to the rice, a ladleful at a time, stirring between each addition to allow the liquid to become completely absorbed. Continue to do this until the rice is cooked *al dente* and all the stock has been absorbed.

4 Add the asparagus, butter and Parmesan cheese, season to taste with salt and freshly ground black pepper, and stir well.

5 Serve with a drizzle of olive oil. Offer extra grated Parmesan cheese to sprinkle on top (optional).

RADICCHIO RISOTTO

1 head radicchio, sliced (save
 some for a garnish)
4 cups chicken or vegetable stock
3 tbsp butter
1 small onion, finely chopped
Salt and pepper
2 cups Arborio rice
1 cup dry white wine
½ cup mascarpone
¼ cup grated Parmesan cheese

Serves 4–6

1 In a medium pot, bring the stock
to a boil, then reduce the heat,
maintaining a simmer. In a
separate shallow pot set over a
medium heat, melt the butter, add
the onion, season with salt and
pepper, and cook, stirring
occasionally, until the onion is
tender but not colored. Add the
radicchio and cook briefly, stirring
occasionally, until it begins to wilt.

2 Add the rice and stir, ensuring
that each grain is coated with
butter. Add the white wine and
continue to cook, stirring, until the
liquid is absorbed. Add 1 cup of
the stock and cook, stirring, until
the liquid is absorbed. Repeat the

process with a second and
subsequent cups of stock until the
rice, when tasted, is found to
have reached the *al dente* stage
(about 20 minutes).

3 Stir in the mascarpone and most
of the Parmesan cheese, reserving
some to sprinkle over at the end.
Serve immediately, garnished with
the reserved radicchio leaves.

BROWN SHORT-GRAIN RICE

Botanical name: *Oryza sativa*
Family: *Poaceae*

Brown short-grain rice is an unmilled rice variety. Unlike white rice, its bran and germ content remain intact, giving it a nutty flavor with more bite. Brown short-grain rice is more nutritious than white rice as many of the vitamins, oils, fiber and minerals are contained in the outermost layers of the rice grains and are not lost during processing. Its distinctive flavor and texture make it suitable for a number of dishes, including puddings, rice balls (*arancini*), croquettes, paella and risotto.

Unlike white rice, brown short-grain rice has a high-fiber bran coating, which means that it takes longer to cook and needs more water. The addition of butter and salt is optional, but does much to enhance the natural flavor of the finished dish.

Health benefits: Short-grain brown rice contains B-complex vitamins (folate and niacin), also magnesium, phosphorus, potassium, calcium and selenium to keep bones strong and the heart functioning well. Consumption of brown short-grain rice is thought to help prevent cancers, lower (bad) cholesterol, benefit postmenopausal women and reduce the risk of developing type 2 diabetes.

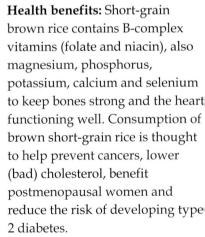

BROWN SHORT-GRAIN RICE WITH BEEF

2–4 tsp vegetable oil
1 beef steak, finely sliced
1 carrot, finely chopped
½ cup bok choy, sliced (optional)
1 red chili, finely sliced
1 green chili, finely sliced
1 tsp grated fresh ginger
2 cloves garlic, crushed
3 cups cooked brown short-grain rice

3 tbsp dark soy sauce
2 tsp dark sesame oil
1 leek, finely sliced

Serves 4–6

1 To a wok or large skillet, add a little of the vegetable oil and brown the steak over a medium heat. Remove with a slotted spoon and set aside.

2 In the same pan, add the rest of the vegetable oil and set it over a medium heat. Add the carrot, bok choy, if using, chilis, ginger and garlic and cook for 2–4 minutes, stirring constantly.

3 Add the beef, cooked rice, soy sauce and sesame oil; mix well. Heat thoroughly for about 5 minutes, stirring constantly. Garnish with the finely sliced leek.

CAMARGUE RED RICE
Botanical name: *Oryza sativa*
Family: *Poaceae*

Camargue red rice, also known as *riz rouge*, is a relatively new variety which has been cultivated since 1988 in the Camargue region of the south of France, a protected marshland area lying between Marseille and Montpellier. Here, the soil is so salty that little else can be grown, but the wetland climate is perfect for rice production in general and has been carried out since the 1800s.

Camargue red rice is brownish-red in color. It is used in its unmilled state and is therefore somewhat earthy and nutty in flavor as well as chewy in texture. It is often cooked in the same way as risotto rice, sautéed in butter first and then water or stock added until the liquid is absorbed.

Like many other unmilled rice varieties, red rice is quite filling so that only a small portion is usually offered. It can be combined with vegetables, nuts and other grains to make a complete meal, or protein, such as fish or meat can be incorporated to make a nutritious main meal. Being in an unmilled state, Camargue red rice has a high nutritive value.

Health benefits: Red rice contains anthocyanin antioxidants, chemicals also present in raspberries, red grapes, eggplant and beets. As with all other rice varieties, red rice is high in vitamins and minerals and its properties make it good for the skin, metabolism, blood pressure and immune system. It is believed to prevent some cancers as well as heart disease.

BELL PEPPER STUFFED WITH GROUND BEEF & CAMARGUE RED RICE

6 red bell peppers
2 tbsp olive oil
½ cup chopped onion
½ cup chopped celery
1 lb ground beef
7 oz canned chopped tomatoes
4 tbsp tomato purée
1 clove garlic, crushed
1 tsp fresh or dried oregano
1 tsp fresh or dried basil
Salt and ground black pepper to
 taste
1½ cups cooked Camargue red rice
1 cup Cheddar cheese, grated

Serves 6

1 Prepare the washed peppers by cutting off their tops and removing the seeds. Place in a large, greased baking pan. Chop the edible parts of the removed tops and set them aside.

2 Heat the olive oil in a large skillet over a medium heat until hot. Sauté the chopped pepper tops, onion and celery for about 5 minutes, or until the vegetables are tender. Add the beef and cook until brown. Add the tomatoes, tomato pureé, garlic, oregano, basil and season well. Leave to simmer for about 10 minutes.

3 Add the cooked rice to the mixture and stir well.

4 Stuff the peppers with the beef/rice mixture almost to the top, then bake at 350°F for 55–65 minutes. If desired, top the peppers with a little grated Cheddar cheese, then return to the oven until the cheese is melted.

SPICY VEGETABLE CAMARGUE RED RICE

1½ tbsp olive oil

1 cup Camargue red rice

1 medium red chili, finely
 chopped

1 medium onion, finely chopped

1 tsp crushed cumin seeds

1 tbsp hot chili sauce

1 tsp smoked paprika

2 cups chicken or vegetable stock

½ cup peas

½ medium can corn kernels,
 drained

Serves 4–6 as a side dish

1 Heat the olive oil on a medium heat in a large skillet. Add the rice, chili, onion and cumin seeds. Stir around for a few minutes until the rice is coated in the oil. Add the hot chili sauce and paprika. Stir through.

2 Add the stock and ½ cup cold water. Bring to a boil, then reduce the heat to low. Cover and simmer for 15 minutes or until the rice has absorbed the liquid and is tender. Just before the end of cooking, add the peas and corn and cook through. Garnish with sprigs of a fresh green herb.

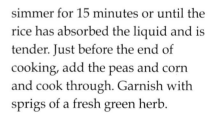

SERVING SUGGESTION: To create a domed effect, pack the rice into a small cup or bowl and turn it out onto a plate.

BROWN LONG-GRAIN RICE

Botanical name: *Oryza sativa*
Family: *Poaceae*

There are several varieties of this type, including American and Basmati. As the name suggests, the grains of this rice are typically longer in length than other varieties. Long-grain rice is relatively easy to cook, in that the grains tend to remain separate rather than clumped together. It is also fluffier when cooked, making it suitable as a side dish or as a base for a sauce. It is commonly used in Indian and Middle Eastern cuisine.

As brown long-grain rice is unmilled, it retains its brownish color with the bran and side hulls remaining intact. Highly

digestable and flavorsome, its unrefined state means that the rice is high in protein, calcium, fiber, magnesium and potassium. It is often used by those wishing to lose weight in that it fills the stomach quickly and gives a feeling of fullness for longer. It is also excellent for diabetics in that its low glycemic rating helps prevent undesirable insulin spikes.

Health benefits: All the brown long-grain rice varieties are high in fiber, rich in vitamins, oils and minerals which benefit health. They also contain antioxidants that help to fight free radicals. Aside from slowing down the aging process, these properties also benefit some diseases such as diabetes by stabilizing blood sugars, and may help prevent infections, some cancers, as well as heart disease.

BROWN LONG-GRAIN RICE PUDDING

⅔ cup brown long-grain rice
1 tsp ground cinnamon
¼ cup runny honey
1 14-oz can light coconut milk
1⅔ cups low-fat milk
1 tsp vanilla extract
A handful of dried cranberries

(It is recommended that a 4–6-qt slow cooker is used to make this dish).

Serves 6

1 Add the rice, cinnamon and sugar to the slow cooker and stir well to combine. Add both milks, mix well, cover, and cook on low for 3-4 hours, or until the rice is tender and the desired thickness has been achieved.

2 When the cooking time is up, add the vanilla and cranberries, stir to combine, cover and leave to rest for about 10 minutes after the slow cooker has been turned off. Serve, garnished with a light sprinkling of cinnamon and a few more cranberries.

PROSO or COMMON MILLET

Botanical name: *Panicum miliaceum*
Family: *Gramineae*

A number of grains come under the term 'millet' but they do not all belong to the same genus, which can be rather misleading. Proso, white or common millet, is a member of the grass family and is obtainable in grocery stores in most countries. While it originated in China, today it is grown commercially throughout the world. In the United States, proso millet is often cultivated to attract gamebirds to hunting fields.

Proso is relatively easy to cultivate and, although it grows well in a variety of climates, it is particularly tolerant of arid conditions. Once considered a grain suitable only for animal or bird feed, it is now gaining popularity as a health food. It can be cooked as a whole grain, flaked or ground into flour, and can be used for bread-making and pasta. It has a sweet, nutty flavor and is very easy to digest, being more alkaline than many cereals; it is a good option for celiacs or those with a gluten intolerance.

When cooked, millet is creamy and looks a little like fluffy rice or mashed potatoes. The grains are tiny in size and round in shape, the most widely available form being the hulled variety, although traditional couscous made from cracked millet can also be found.

Health benefits: Proso millet is high in fiber and so beneficial to those suffering from constipation. It is also said to be helpful in cases of migraine, and contains serotonin, which is mood-calming and said to induce feelings of happiness. It is also of benefit to the cardiovascular system and is one of the most non-allergenic of all the cereals. It is claimed to regulate blood sugars and prevent gallstones, childhood asthma and some cancers.

MILLET PORRIDGE WITH APRICOTS & PRUNES

⅓ cup millet
½ cup water
½ cup milk
½ cup sugar
½ tsp vanilla extract
Pinch of salt
Dried apricots and prunes

Serves 1

1 Soak the apricots and prunes in water for at least one hour or overnight. (To speed the softening process, use hot water.) Cook the fruit in the water in which they were soaked over a medium-high heat until they become plump and yield easily when pierced with a fork.

2 In a small pot, combine the millet, water, milk, sugar, vanilla and salt. Bring to a boil, then reduce the heat, cover, and simmer for 25 minutes. Cook for 3–5 minutes longer, partially covered, if some liquid remains.

3 Drain the fruit and stir into the porridge. A drizzle of maple syrup or honey makes a good addition.

VEGETABLE SOUP WITH MILLET

2 tbsp olive oil

1 onion, chopped

1 stick celery, chopped

2 carrots, chopped

1 leek, chopped

1 turnip, peeled and cut into
 bite-sized chunks

1 sweet potato, cut into bite-sized
 chunks

1 bay leaf

1 tbsp chopped fresh thyme

1 qt vegetable stock

2 cups water

1 cup millet

Salt and freshly ground pepper

Sage leaves to garnish

Serves 6–8

1 Warm the olive oil over a medium heat in a large pot. Add the onion, celery, carrots and leek and cook for 5 minutes until soft but not browned.

2 Add the turnip, sweet potato, bay leaf, chopped thyme, stock and water, and season well. Bring to a boil, cover, then reduce the heat and leave to simmer for 15 minutes or so.

3 Meanwhile, heat a small skillet over a medium heat. Add the millet and toast it for 5 minutes until golden, stirring frequently.

4 Add the millet to the soup and leave to simmer for an additional 20 minutes or so until both millet and vegetables are tender. Remove the bay leaf, adjust the seasoning, and serve, garnished with fresh sage leaves.

RYE

Botanical name: *Secale cereale*
Family: *Poaceae*

Rye is the fifth most important cereal grown throughout the world, exceeded only by corn, oats, wheat and rice. Rye belongs to the grass family, being closely related to wheat and barley, and is intensively grown as a grain. It is also used as a cover crop and also for animal feed.

There are many rye varieties, used to make flour for rye bread and crispbreads, also beer, while certain varieties are exclusively used in the distillation of whiskeys and vodkas.

Rye can be eaten whole, either as boiled rye berries or in a rolled form similar to rolled oats. It is difficult to mill, with the result that much of the germ and bran remain intact, producing the rich, hearty taste. Full of fiber, rye has exceptional water-binding properties. It is a great food when trying to lose weight, in that it is very satisfying and maintains a feeling of fullness for longer.

Rye was first domesticated relatively recently, having first

been cultivated in Germany in around 400 BC, having evolved from a wild species of grass that grew as a weed in crop fields. Today, rye is most popular in Scandinavian and Eastern European countries, where it occupies an important position in food culture. It is widely grown commercially in the Russian Federation, Poland, China, Denmark and Canada. Rye is also beneficial to the environment, in that it reduces soil erosion and, when used as a cover crop, enhances soil water retention. It also helps to control weed growth, reducing the need for herbicides.

Health benefits: Rye makes a good contribution to cardiovascular health, reduces atherosclerosis, lowers (bad) cholesterol and is of benefit to diabetics. It is said to prevent certain types of cancers, asthma and is an aid in the pursuit of weight reduction. It also contains many health-giving key components, such as fiber, manganese, copper, magnesium, phosphorus, B-complex vitamins and phenolic antioxidants.

RUSSIAN BLACK RYE BREAD

2½ cups warm water
2 packages dried yeast
¼ cup butter
¼ cup white vinegar
¼ cup blackstrap molasses
1 oz unsweetened chocolate, melted
2 tsp salt
1 tbsp fennel seeds
2 tsp instant coffee granules (optional)
4¼ cups wheat bread flour
5 cups rye flour
¾ cup dates, finely chopped (optional)

Makes 2 loaves

1 Put half a cup of warm water into a large warmed bowl. Sprinkle in the yeast and stir the two together, using your fingers, until the yeast is fully dissolved. Add the remaining water, the butter, vinegar, molasses, chocolate (melted in a microwave oven for 30 seconds), salt and fennel seeds. (Many also like to add 2 tsp instant coffee granules at this stage).

2 Slowly stir in the wheat flour, blend well, then stir in the rye flour and mix together to make a soft dough.

3 Place the ball of dough on a lightly floured surface. Cover with a clean, damp cloth and leave to rest for 15 minutes, then knead the dough until it becomes smooth and elastic (about 10–15 minutes). Put the dough ball into a lightly oiled bowl, turning it so that the underside also becomes covered with a thin film of oil. Cover the bowl and leave the dough in a warm place until it has doubled its size (about 1–1½ hours).

4 When fully risen, punch the dough down, then turn it out onto a lightly floured surface.

If using, knead the chopped dates into the dough, distributing them evenly, then cut the dough into equal halves. Shape each half into balls, then place each ball into greased 8-inch round cake pans or put them onto a large oiled sheet pan. Cover, then leave again to rise until doubled in size (about 1 hour).

5 Meanwhile, the oven can be preheated to 350°F. Bake the loaves for 45 minutes or until they sound hollow when tapped. Remove from the pans and leave to cool on wire racks.

HONEY, PECAN & RYE CAKE

1 cup all-purpose flour
1 cup medium rye flour
¼ cup chopped pecans
¼ cup pecans, left whole
⅔ cup honey
⅔ cup granulated sugar
¼ cup canola oil
2 large eggs
2 tsp baking soda
1 tsp ground cinnamon
½ tsp ground nutmeg
¼ tsp ground ginger
½ tsp salt
¼ cup water

Serves 6–8

1 Preheat the oven to 275°F. Grease and flour a medium-sized bread pan.

2 With an electric mixer set on a low speed (or mix by hand), thoroughly combine all the ingredients, retaining some of the chopped and whole pecan nuts for the final decoration.

3 Pour the mixture into the pan and bake for about 75 minutes or until a skewer, when inserted into the cake, comes out clean.

4 Leave to cool completely in the pan, then turn out and decorate the top of the cake with the reserved chopped and whole pecans.

FREEKEH

Botanical name: *Triticum aestivum*
Family: *Poaceae*

Freekeh, also called farik or fireek, is a cereal food made from green wheat that has been harvested when immature, then put through a roasting process in its production. Its origin is the Middle East, where it is commonly eaten in the Levant, the Arabian Peninsula, Palestine, Egypt and in some of the North African countries.

The wheat is harvested while the grains are yellow and the seeds are still soft; it is then piled and sun-dried. The piles are then carefully set on fire so that only the straw and chaff burn and not the seeds. (It is the high moisture content of the seeds that prevents them from burning.) The now roasted wheat then undergoes further thrashing and sun-drying to make the flavor, texture and color uniform. It is this thrashing or rubbing process that gives the food its name, meaning 'rubbed.' The seeds are now cracked into smaller pieces so that they resemble green bulgur.

The history of freekeh dates back to around 2300 BC, when it is believed that an Eastern Mediterranean nation was anticipating an attack from a neighboring country. The people were so worried about losing their crops that they harvested them early and stored them away. But the young wheat was burned when their city finally did come under attack, after which it was discovered that it remained fit to eat. Today this process is still used and, despite this odd treatment, freekeh can claim many nutritional benefits.

Health benefits: Modern reseachers have found that green wheat has a number of health benefits. It is naturally low in carbohydrates and high in fiber, both considered helpful in achieving weight loss. Its fiber content is also of benefit to those suffering from irritable bowl syndrome (IBS). Freekeh also has probiotic effects, is good for eye health, and helps regulate blood sugars. It is also said to prevent some cancers and is thought to be an aid to concentration. Freekeh is rich in calcium, iron and zinc.

FREEKEH TABOULI

1 cup cooked freekeh
¼ cup extra virgin olive oil
1 clove garlic, crushed and finely
 chopped
1 tbsp fresh lemon juice
¼ cup finely chopped fresh parsley
¼ cup finely chopped fresh mint
 leaves
¼ cup finely chopped basil leaves
3 scallions, finely chopped
16 grape tomatoes, quartered

Salt and freshly ground black
 pepper

Serves 2

1 Cook the freekeh according to
the packaging instructions. Drain
well and set aside to cool to room
temperature. Make a dressing
with the olive oil, garlic and
lemon juice in a medium-sized
bowl.

2 Add the freekeh, parsley, mint,
basil, scallions and tomatoes to the
bowl and mix well. Season
generously with salt and black
pepper.

3 Leave to stand for a little before
serving to allow the flavors to
mingle and mature.

WHEAT

Botanical name: *Triticum aestivum*
Family: *Poaceae*

Wheat originated in the Levant region of the Near East but is now cultivated worldwide. It is the third most important cereal in the world after rice and maize. Globally, it is the leading source of vegetable protein in human food.

Wheat production began some 8,000 years ago when human settlements first flourished. Bread wheat is known to have been grown in the Nile valley by 5000 BC and in the Euphrates and Tigris valleys by 4000 BC, spreading to China by 2500 BC and later to England by 2000 BC. Wheat was first grown in the United States in 1602 on an island off the Massachusetts coast. Today, the world leaders in wheat production are China, India, the United States, France and Russia, and wheat is grown on more land worldwide than any other crop. It is well suited to harsh environments and is mostly grown in windswept areas that are too dry and too cold for the more tropically inclined rice or maize.

Although wheat can be fed to livestock it is more important as a human food source, being nutritious, concentrated and easily stored and processed. Unlike any other plant-derived food, wheat contains gluten protein, which enables a leavened dough, made from the flour, to rise by forming minute gas cells that hold carbon dioxide during fermentation, thus

producing a light and textured bread. Wheat is a major ingredient of many of our foods and is used in the manufacturing of breads, cakes, cookies, pastries, pastas and breakfast foods, etc.

Health benefits: Wheat is important in the quest for healthy living, in that it is known to reduce the risk of heart disease and to lower (bad) cholesterol, due to its comparatively low fat content; it also helps in diabetes in that it serves to regulate blood sugar levels.

All parts of the grain kernel, including the germ, bran and endosperm, are valuable. As with many other grains, it is best to eat it in its whole form to ensure the

maximum nutrient content is preserved. Whole wheat contains B-complex vitamins, calcium, phosphorus, folic acid, copper, zinc, iron and fiber, properties which make it an important food source and staple for all-round general health.

WHOLE WHEAT PASTA WITH SUN-DRIED TOMATOES & OLIVES

1 lb whole wheat tagliatelle
1 clove garlic, finely chopped
⅓ cup extra virgin olive oil
Zest and juice of 1 large lemon
1 cup sun-dried tomatoes in oil,
 drained and chopped
1 cup pitted and sliced olives (use
 black or green or a mixture of
 both)
¾ cup Parmesan cheese shavings

Serves 4–6

1 Bring a large pot of salted water
to a boil over a high heat. Add the
pasta and cook (stirring
occasionally) until tender
but still firm to the bite (8–10
minutes).

2 While the pasta is cooking,
mix the garlic with the oil, lemon
zest and lemon juice in a
separate bowl.

3 Drain the cooked pasta and
return it to the pot, add the oil and
lemon mixture, then add the
tomatoes and olives. Mix all the
ingredients together, checking the
seasoning, and serve in individual
bowls, garnished generously with
shavings of Parmesan cheese.

WHOLE WHEAT BANANA MUFFINS

3½ cups whole wheat flour
2 tsp baking soda
1 tsp salt
⅔ cup canola or vegetable oil
1 cup honey
4 eggs
2 cups mashed ripe banana
½ cup hot water

Makes 24 muffins

1 In a large mixing bowl, stir together the dry ingredients.

2 In a smaller bowl, beat the oil and honey together, then add the eggs and beat well. Stir in the mashed banana until the ingredients are thoroughly incorporated.

3 Gradually add the hot water, mixing well after each addition.

4 Spoon the mixture into muffin cups, then bake at 325°F for 15 minutes, or until the muffins are golden brown. To test if cooked, pierce a muffin with a skewer which should come out dry. Place the muffins on a rack to cool.

FARRO

Botanical name: *Triticum dicoccum*
Family: *Poaceae*

Farro is a type of wheat and was one of the first plants to be domesticated in the Middle East by the ancient Egyptians around 6,000 years ago. As a low-yield crop, farro has largely fallen out of favor over the centuries and replaced with other crops, although it is still popular in Italy.

There is some confusion and debate as to what farro actually is. In Italy, spelt *(Triticum spelta)*, emmer *(Triticum dicoccum)* and einkorn *(Triticum monococcum)* are all called farro, although emmer is by far the most commonly grown farro in the Garfagnana region of Tuscany, where it has been designated *Indicazione Geografica Protetta* which, by law, guarantees its geographic integrity.

In Italy, farro is often eaten in the form of whole grains in soups and breads. It can also be made into pasta, this being less common in that the texture is considered unattractive by some.

Outside Italy, farro is considered to be a health food by

many and can only be sourced in specialist shops. It usually comes in its dried form, but needs to be thoroughly boiled and softened before consumption. In fact, the grains are so tough that overnight soaking is advisable. When perfectly cooked, the grain should be soft on the inside but still a little crunchy on the outside.

Health benefits: Farro is a great source of vitamin B3, which is essential for the metabolism. It is also packed with fiber, making it an aid to digestion and useful in weight-loss regimes in that it maintains a feeling of fullness for longer. It is also claimed to help prevent diabetes, cardiovascular disease and moderates (bad) cholesterol. It is also rich in protein and antioxidants and contains good amounts of zinc and iron.

ITALIAN FARRO SOUP

3 tbsp extra virgin olive oil
1 Spanish onion, thinly sliced
2 celery sticks, thinly sliced
1 leek, thinly sliced
1 cup pearled farro
1 cup canned borlotti beans,
 strained and washed
½ tbsp tomato paste
2 tomatoes, finely chopped
2 crimini mushrooms, finely
 chopped
1 large carrot, finely chopped
Salt and freshly ground black
 pepper
Freshly grated Parmesan cheese

Serves 4

1 In a medium to large pot or casserole dish, heat the olive oil over a medium-high heat. Add the onion, celery and leek and sauté, stirring occasionally, until the vegetables are soft and translucent, but do not brown.

2 Add the farro, beans, tomato paste, tomatoes, mushrooms and carrot, stirring so that the tomato paste is spread evenly throughout the pot. Add sufficient water to cover the mixture completely.

3 Bring to a boil, then lower the heat and leave the soup to simmer gently for about 1 hour until the farro is tender, adding more water if necessary.

4 Season well with salt and black pepper and serve the soup with grated Parmesan cheese sprinkled over (optional).

FARRO RISOTTO WITH PORCINI

1 cup dried porcini mushrooms
5½ cups chicken or vegetable stock
2 tbsp extra virgin olive oil
1½ cups pearled farro
½ cup finely chopped onion
1 clove garlic, chopped
½ cup dry white wine
1 tsp chopped fresh thyme
Salt
½ tsp freshly ground black pepper
¼ cup grated Parmesan
 cheese

Serves 4-6

1 Place the dried mushrooms in a medium bowl, cover with boiling water and leave to stand for 30 minutes or until tender; drain. Finely chop the mushrooms.

2 Heat the stock in a separate pot (do not boil), keeping it warm over a very low heat.

3 To a large skillet, add the oil and heat it up. Add the farro and the onion and sauté for 5 minutes, stirring occasionally. Add the garlic and cook for 1 minute more, stirring constantly. Add the

porcini mushrooms and ½ teaspoon salt. Cook for a further 5 minutes, stirring occasionally. Add the wine and chopped thyme and cook until the liquid is almost entirely evaporated.

4 Add a ladleful of the hot stock to the risotto and continue cooking it until the liquid is absorbed. Repeat the process until the stock is used up and the farro is tender

(about 40 minutes, but a little extra stock may be needed if the farro has not softened within that time).

5 Taste, adding a little more salt if necessary, some pepper, and the Parmesan cheese, stirring it into the risotto. Serve the risotto garnished with a sprig of fresh thyme.

DURUM WHEAT

Botanical name: *Triticum durum*
Family: *Poaceae*

Durum wheat, also known as macaroni wheat, is an important crop cultivated in many parts of the world for its main use in pasta-making, a staple food of Italy, in particular, for as long as anyone can remember.

Durum wheat was developed by artificial selection of the domesticated emmer wheat, which evolved a naked, free-threshing form. In Latin, *durum* means 'hard,' and it is this exceptional strength that makes it suitable for pasta. Not only is it used in the production of pasta and pizza dough in Italy, but also in breadmaking, although rarely from 100 per cent durum which is low in the desirable gluten required to give the bread its elasticity. An example of pure durum wheat bread is the *pagnotte di enna* or *rimacinato* bread of Sicily, and it is also used in Arab countries in the making of *tabouli*, *kishk*, *kibba* and *bitfun*.

Dried pasta is produced on a massive scale and is almost exclusively made from durum

These have antioxidant properties that protect the body from many diseases. Durum wheat contains calcium, potassium and iron, which are important nutrients for protecting the body against a number of conditions. Durum is a good source of B-complex vitamins and also vitamin E, which strengthens the immune system. Durum wheat is good for diabetics, in that it slows the digestion and helps to regulate blood sugar levels.

semolina (the hard grains left after the milling of flour). Home-made fresh pastas also use durum wheat but sometimes they are mixed with softer wheats. Most of the durum wheat grown nowadays is amber durum, the grains of which have a yellow endosperm which produces the distinctive color.

Health benefits: Durum wheat is exceptionally rich in protein, making it ideal for vegetarians. It is also high in carbohydrates which are rich in phytonutrients.

HOW TO MAKE PIZZA

14 oz strong bread flour
3½ oz semolina flour, plus extra
 for dusting
2 tsp salt
1½ tsp dried yeast
1 cup lukewarm water
3 tbsp olive oil

Makes 2 pizza bases

1 In a large mixing bowl, stir together the flour, semolina and salt. Stir in the dried yeast. Make a well in the center of the flour mixture and pour in most of the water along with the olive oil. Bring the dough together with your hands, adding the remaining water if the dough feels tight or hard. Turn the dough out onto a clean surface and knead for 10 minutes or until it becomes smooth and elastic.

2 Shape the dough into a ball and place in an oiled bowl. Cover with a damp cloth and leave to prove in a warm place for about 1-1½ hours, or until the dough has doubled in size.

3 Remove the dough ball from the bowl and knock the air out. Cut the dough into two equal portions, shaping each portion into a ball. Cover the balls with a damp cloth and leave to prove again for about 15 minutes.

4 Place a pizza stone or upturned sheet pan into the oven and preheat it to its highest setting. Dust the work surface liberally with semolina, then roll out one of the balls to form a circle. Spread the surface with 1 tbsp tomato sauce and the toppings of your choice.

5 Slide the pizza onto the pizza stone and cook for 8–10 minutes or until the base is golden-brown and the toppings bubbling. Repeat with the other half of the dough.

HOW TO MAKE FRESH PASTA

1¼ lbs durum wheat flour or
Italian Tipo '00' flour
6 large eggs, at room temperature

Serves 4

(It is recommended that you read the instructions that came with your pasta machine before commencing.)

1 Heap the flour in a mound on top of the counter, then make a well in the flour and crack in the eggs. Using your fingers, gradually draw the flour into the center, mixing it lightly with the eggs until a pliable dough forms.

2 Knead the dough, using the heel of your hand, for at least three minutes until it is very smooth. Wrap the dough in plastic film and leave it to sit at room temperature for an hour.

3 Divide the dough into six or eight pieces then, working one piece at a time, fashion them into rough rectangles before passing them through your pasta machine on the widest setting. Fold each piece of dough in half or thirds and pass through again, then fold and pass through one more time.

4 Continue passing the pasta pieces through the machine, closing down the opening of the rollers a few notches with each pass until the desired thickness is achieved. (Dust them very lightly with flour if the dough is sticking.) Then use the pasta cutter attachment to cut the sheets into the type of pasta required, i.e., pappadelle, tagliatelle, fettucini, etc., or use a knife to cut the pasta by hand into the strands or shapes you require.

5 Spread out the pasta to dry on a clean cloth before cooking it in boiling, well-salted water for no more than 6 or 7 minutes.

SPELT

Botanical name: *Triticum spelta*
Family: *Poaceae*

Spelt, also known as dinkel or hulled wheat, is an ancient species of wheat cultivated for thousands of years. The earliest archeological evidence of its existence is from the fifth millennium BC in Transcaucasia, north-east of the Black Sea.

Spelt is thought to be the original wheat species used in the making of bread, and was an important staple food during the Bronze and Middle Ages in Europe. Spelt (*Triticum spelta*) is a grain related to common bread wheat (*Triticum sativum*) but has certain properties which, in many respects, makes it quite different.

Having fallen from favor as a grain for cultivation in the 19th

century, following the rapid development in modern farming techniques, spelt is currently enjoying a resurgence in popularity as information about its value as a food source and its ability to be tolerated by many with wheat sensitivities becomes more widely known. Spelt bread is also starting to find its way into some specialist bakeries, being slightly sweet and nutty in flavor and similar in appearance to rye bread.

In Germany, spelt loaves and rolls (*dinkelbrot*) are widely available. In grain form, spelt makes a good substitute for rice or potatoes.

Health benefits: Spelt reduces the risk of atherosclerosis, cardiovascular disease and build-up of (bad) cholesterol, and helps prevent gallstones, childhood asthma and some cancers. It protects against diabetes, obesity and stroke, and is high in fiber and many important vitamins and minerals.

SPELT & OAT CAKE WITH CRANBERRIES

2 cups whole grain spelt flour
1 cup oats, plus a little extra for
 sprinkling
2 tsp baking powder
½ tsp bicarbonate of soda
½ tsp salt
1 cup natural yogurt
1 egg
¼ cup melted coconut oil
¼ cup honey
¾ cup milk
½ cup fresh cranberries

Makes 1 loaf

1 Preheat the oven to 375°F. Mix all the dry ingredients together in a medium-sized bowl.

2 Mix all the wet ingredients together in a smaller bowl.

3 Add the wet ingredients to the dry ones and mix until just combined.

4 Mix the cranberries with a little flour to prevent them from sinking to the bottom of the cake, then fold them gently into the cake mix.

5 Oil a small loaf pan and pour in the cake mixture. Sprinkle a few more oats on top to decorate, then bake for 35–45 minutes or until a skewer, inserted into the cake, comes out clean.

FETA SALAD WITH SPELT

1½ cups whole grain spelt
4½ cups water
1 tbsp white wine vinegar
1 tbsp olive oil
Salt and freshly gound black
  pepper
1½ cups halved grape tomatoes
2 handfuls arugula
½ cup diced feta cheese

Serves 4–6

1 Add the spelt to the water in a large pot and bring to a boil. Reduce the heat to low and simmer, uncovered, until all the water is absorbed and the grain is tender (about 1 hour).

2 Drain the spelt, rinse with cold water, then refrigerate for at least 1 hour or overnight.

3 Whisk together the wine vinegar, oil, salt and pepper. Add to the cold spelt and mix thoroughly. Add the grape tomatoes and gently fold them in.

4 Make a bed of arugula on a serving dish, pile on the spelt and tomatoes, and sprinkle over the feta cheese.

KHORASAN WHEAT

Botanical name: *Triticum turanicum*
Family: *Poaceae*

Khorasan wheat derives its name from the historic region that lies mostly in parts of modern-day Iran, Turkmenistan and Afghanistan. The precise origin of this wheat is unknown, although scientists believe it was first discovered in western Anatolia (Turkey in Asia).

Khorasan or Oriental wheat is known for its distinctive nutty flavor and large grain size, apart from which it resembles very closely the common wheat *(Triticum aestivum)*, although the grains have a distinctive amber color and high vitreousness.

It is in relatively recent times that Khorasan wheat has gained in popularity as a health food whose genetic properties have not been compromised by hybridization or genetic modification. It is pesticide-resistant, when compared with other wheats, and is therefore suitable for organic and sustainable cultivation.

Khorasan wheat can be used as a whole grain in flour, pasta and cereals, and makes a good substitute for barley or bulgur. Khorasan wheat has higher nutritional values when compared with modern wheats.

Health benefits: Khorasan wheat is high in lipids and is therefore considered to be a high-energy grain when compared with other wheats. It is rich in proteins and vitamins A and B-complex. It is a good source of fiber and minerals such as calcium, iron, phosphorus, potassium, copper, manganese, magnesium, selenium and zinc. It is high in antioxidants, boosts the body's immunity, lowers (bad) cholesterol, prevents some cancers and aids digestion. It is also important for cardiovascular health, protects against diabetes and is of help to those wishing to lose weight.

AFGHAN STUFFED SQUASH

3 tbsp vegetable oil
½ cup diced onion
1 garlic clove, minced
¼ lb ground lamb
Salt and pepper to taste
1 tbsp tomato paste
¼ cup water
2 butternut squashes
¼ cup cooked Khorasan wheat
¼ cup cooked split peas
1 tsp dried tarragon
2 tsp advieh* (optional)
1 cup diced goat's cheese

Serves 4

1 In a large skillet, fry the onion in the oil, then add the garlic and the ground lamb. Season well and continue cooking until the meat is lightly browned. Add the tomato paste with the ¼ cup of water, then simmer on a low heat until all the juices are absorbed.

2 Cut the squashes in half lengthways, remove and discard the seeds, then carve out the flesh, chopping it up and setting it aside for later. Sprinkle the insides of the squash halves with salt.

3 In a bowl, mix together the wheat, split peas, meat mixture, tarragon, advieh and the chopped squash. Check seasonings. Load the mixture into the squash skins.

4 In an overproof casserole, bring 1 cup of water to a boil. Place the squash halves in the water, cover the pan with a lid, and bake in an oven preheated to 375°F for 45 minutes or until a fork easily penetrates the skin.

5 Remove the lid and sprinkle the halves with the diced goat's cheese. Place the half-squashes under a preheated broiler until the cheese starts to melt. Garnish with flat-leaf parsley and serve.

* Advieh is a spice mix used in Iranian cuisine.

96

CORN/MAIZE

Botanical name: *Zea mays*
Family: *Poaceae*

Corn, also known in some Anglophone countries as maize, is a large grain plant domesticated by indigenous peoples in Mesoamerica in prehistoric times, before which time it grew wild in Mexico. It was quite different from the corn grown today. Over the centuries the Olmec and the Mayans cultivated numerous varieties and eventually the crop spread throughout the Americas. During the 15th and 16th centuries, European traders and explorers carried corn back to Europe, where it was introduced as a crop in many countries. Today corn is the most popular grain crop grown throughout the Americas.

There are more than 100 subspecies and varieties of corn, some of which are quite familiar and often yellow or cream in color. The kernel of the corn plant is the part which is usually eaten and the part that holds the most

nutrients. Depending upon where the corn is grown, and the variety, there are different kinds which can produce pink, blue, purple or black kernels.

Corn can be cooked either with or without its husk in a variety of ways. Corn flour is used to make a highly palatable bread which is easily broken down in the body. It can also be made into tortillas and polenta. Corn kernels can be sautéed, made into salads, broiled, made into popcorn, porridge or added to stews and soups.

Corn is rich in carbohydrates, making it a good source of energy

which is released slowly, keeping the body active for longer. Corn is a useful aid for those wishing to gain weight, in that it has a high calorific content, and it has become a staple for survival in some agriculture-based countries.

Health benefits: Corn is not only high in fiber, but it is also loaded

with vitamins and minerals. It is a good source of vitamins A, B and E, and is rich in phytochemicals

which afford the body good protection against a number of diseases. Minerals in corn include phosphorus, magnesium, manganese, zinc, iron and copper, nutrients known to protect the heart, prevent anemia, lower (bad) cholesterol and help control type 2 diabetes and high blood pressure.

CHINESE CHICKEN & SWEETCORN SOUP

6 cups chicken stock
1 large chicken breast fillet
¼ cup finely diced carrots
10 oz canned corn kernels
1 tbsp cornstarch
2 tbsp light soy sauce
2 eggs, beaten
Salt and pepper to taste

Serves 4

1 Bring the stock to a boil in a large pot, add the chicken breast and carrot, then poach gently until the chicken is cooked through.

2 Remove the chicken breast from the stock and leave it to cool for a few minutes before shredding it.

3 Add the corn to the stock and bring back to a boil over a medium heat. (Keep a little corn back for a garnish, if you wish.)

4 Mix the cornstarch and soy sauce into a paste, then stir it into the soup to thicken it slightly. Add the shredded chicken.

5 Pour the beaten eggs into the soup in a steady stream, stirring constantly with a fork. (The egg will cook in the soup, forming atttractive strands.) Season according to taste, and serve topped with corn kernels and fresh parsley sprigs.

NECTARINE POLENTA CAKE

⅓ cup softened butter
⅔ cup sugar
2 large eggs
¼ cup milk
½ tsp grated lemon zest
1 tbsp lemon juice
1⅔ cups all-purpose flour
¼ cup yellow polenta (cornmeal)
1 tsp baking powder
¼ tsp baking soda
Salt
4 firm, medium-sized nectarines, halved and pitted
1 tbsp sugar for topping

Serves 8

1 Preheat the oven to 350°F. In a large bowl, mix together the butter and sugar until pale and fluffy. Add the eggs, one at a time, beating well after each addition. Add the milk, lemon zest and mix well. Then add the lemon juice. Fold in the flour, polenta, baking powder, baking soda and a pinch of salt, and mix lightly until smooth.

2 Grease and line a 9-inch square cake pan, then pour in the cake mixture. Slice the nectarine halves into eighths, then place the slices evenly on top of the cake mixture, sprinkling over a little sugar. Bake for 28 minutes or until a skewer, inserted into the center of the cake, comes out clean. Cool in the pan before turning out and cutting into squares.

WILD RICE

Botanical name: *Zizania aquatica*
Family: *Poaceae*

Technically, wild rice is not a rice at all but a seed from a marsh grass, and much of it sold in the world today consists of cultivated rather than wild varieties. The type that is truly wild and uncultivated is obtainable, but only from specialist sources.

Wild rice (*Zizania aquatica*) is an annual aquatic seed found mostly in the uppermost freshwater lakes of North America, particularly in the Great Lake region of Minnesota. About 80 per cent of wild rice grown in the United States today is cultivated in paddies. There are two other varieties of wild rice that exist and both are grown in Asia. They are usually consumed as vegetables rather than as grains.

There are three principal grades of wild rice: giant or long-grain (which is the finest quality), fancy or medium-grain and, finally, select or short-grain, which is more suitable for soups and casseroles. When cooked, wild rice has a rich, nutty flavor, and is

delightfully chewy, the grains being noticeably more elongated than usual rice grains. It can be cooked in stock for extra flavor, and goes well with fruits, vegetables and nuts.

Wild rice is a perfect food, in that it is low in fat and calories while being high in protein and fiber, making it great for weight-loss programs. Wild rice is more loaded with nutrients than ordinary rice.

Health benefits: Wild rice is a good source of the B-complex vitamins, folic acid, fiber and carbohydrates. It is also rich in magnesium, phosphorus, zinc, manganese, and also contains calcium and iron. It is gluten-free, making it a useful food for individuals intolerant of gluten. The consumption of wild rice is of benefit to the eyes, skin, hair, stomach, intestines, nervous system and liver.

WILD RICE WITH BLACK LENTILS

12 oz uncooked wild rice
2½ cups chicken or vegetable stock
4 oz uncooked black beluga lentils
1 cup water
1 small onion, cut into fine rounds
1 tbsp vegetable oil
1 tbsp olive oil
Salt and pepper to taste

Serves 4 as a side dish

1 WILD RICE: In a pot, combine the wild rice with the stock and stir. Bring to a boil, then lower the heat, cover, and simmer for 50–60 minutes. Drain the rice, reserving any remaining stock.

2 BLACK LENTILS: In another pot, mix the lentils with the water and bring to a boil, then simmer for about 10 minutes. Drain, cover, and set aside.

3 Meanwhile, gently fry the onion in the vegetable oil until it is crisp and golden.

4 Mix together the cooked rice, lentils and olive oil, adding some of the reserved stock if the mixture seems too dry. Season to taste. Serve topped with the fried onions.

SEEDS

CHAPTER TWO

SEEDS

MUSTARD SEED
Botanical name: *Brassica hirta/Sinapis alba, B. juncea, B. nigra*
Family: *Brassicaceae*

The mustard plant is a member of the *Brassicaceae* family, related to broccoli, Brussels sprouts and cabbage, etc. Not only is it used throughout the world as a culinary seasoning, but it also has useful medicinal applications. The small, round seeds of the various mustard plants range from yellowish white to black in color, and come from three different plants: white mustard (*B. hirta/S. alba),* brown Indian mustard (*B. juncea*), and black mustard (*B. nigra*). Black mustard seeds are the strongest-tasting, producing a hot, lively taste, while the white seeds, which are actually yellow in color, are a good deal milder and are used to make yellow mustard pastes such as Dijon and Meaux.

The mustard plant has its roots in Europe and Asia, with the white variety coming from the

Health benefits: Mustard seeds are low in calories and have nutritional value, being an important source of microelements. The seeds can also be processed to make an oil that is used in aromatherapy and massage, and which is said to promote luxuriant hair growth and glowing skin. Mustard seeds contain vitamin E, selenium, potassium, fatty acids, calcium, phosphorus and iron.

Mediterranean and the black from the Middle East. The seeds are believed to have been popular in ancient Greece and Rome, where both civilizations used them for medicinal purposes and in cooking. The word mustard comes from the Latin *mustum ardens* or 'burning must;' the plant is one of the most widely cultivated spices in the world today.

107

WHOLE GRAIN MUSTARD

2 tbsp white mustard seeds
2 tbsp brown mustard seeds
½ cup dry white wine or cider
 vinegar
½ tsp salt
1 tsp sugar

Makes 1 small jar

1 Place the mustard seeds in a non-metallic container, such as a glass or ceramic bowl, and cover them with the wine or vinegar. Leave to stand, covered with plastic film, for 3 days, but do not refrigerate.

2 Check the seeds from time to time when it will be noticed that they will have swollen as they absorb the liquid. Add more liquid, if necessary, to prevent drying out. After 3 days, drain of the surplus liquid and reserve.

3 Use a food processor or pestle and mortar to very briefly blend the seeds, then add the salt and sugar and blend again, adding some of the reserved liquid if necessary. (You will notice that the

lighter seeds will break down easily to a creamy texture while the darker ones, being harder, will stay relatively whole.)

4 Put the mustard into a sterilized glass jar and leave it to mature for a couple of days before using. Refrigerate, once opened, and use within 1 month.

NOTE: Freshly chopped herbs, garlic, horseradish or ground sweet spices, such as cloves, cinnamon, allspice or cardamom, may be added as an extra flavoring but will shorten the shelf life of the mustard, which should be used up as soon as possible.

MUSTARD & CHILI POTATOES

8–10 medium-sized waxy potatoes
3 tbsp olive oil
3 medium-sized chilis, deseeded
 and finely sliced
1 tbsp whole grain mustard
1 tsp sesame seeds
Lemon wedges

Serves 4

1 Peel and cut the potatoes into wedges. Bring them to a boil in a pot of salted water, then lower the heat to a simmer until they are cooked through but not falling apart.

2 In a small skillet, heat the oil and sauté the chilis gently (don't let them burn). Turn down the heat and stir in the whole grain mustard and sesame seeds.

3 Drain the potatoes and return them to their pot. Pour the contents of the skillet into the potatoes and stir gently to mix.

4 Transfer the potatoes to a serving dish and serve with lemon wedges.

HEMP SEED

Botanical name: *Cannabis sativa*
Family: *Cannabaceae*

The hemp plant is one of the oldest of the cultivated crops, with a usage that can be traced back to 8000 BC to China and the Middle East. Hemp is a commonly used term for high-growing varieties of the cannabis plant and its products, which include fiber, oil, and seed. Hemp is refined into products such as hemp seed foods, hemp oil, wax, resin, rope, cloth, pulp, paper and fuel. Interestingly, the word 'canvas', a material used in sail-making, derives from hemp's botanical name, *cannabis*.

This highly industrial plant must not be confused with its potent cousin, *Cannabis indica*, otherwise known as marijuana, the legality of which varies from country to country.

The seeds of *C. sativa* are among the most highly nutritious of the seeds available to us as food, in that they contain a concentrated balance of many important vitamins, minerals and other nutrients, and it is only relatively recently that the seeds have been rediscovered as a gluten-free 'superfood.' Not only do they provide valuable health benefits, but they also taste good, while hemp seed products are generally considered to be more allergy-free than those from many other plants.

Hemp seeds can be used in cooking and baking to add a nutty flavor to all kinds of recipes. Routinely adding them to your food is a great way of improving your dietary health as a whole.

Health benefits: Hemp seeds have a wide spectrum of health benefits. They are a source of concentrated essential fats, complete proteins, enzymes and vitamins, but are low in saturated fat. The nutritional properties of hemp seeds play many roles in neurological functioning, oxygen transfer, and cardiovascular maintenance, for example. The seeds are also thought to relieve premenstral tension and their antioxidant qualities are particularly good for the skin, hair and bones.

RIGHT: Hemp seeds which have been hulled.

111

EGGPLANT & ZUCCHINI ROLLS WITH HEMP SEEDS

4 zucchini (courgettes)
4 small eggplants (aubergines)
1½ cups grated Parmesan cheese
½ tbsp virgin olive oil
1½ tsp hemp seeds
Salt and freshly ground black
 pepper
Parsley

Serves 4–6

1 Preheat the oven to 375°F.
Wash, then slice the eggplants and zucchini into thin strips.

2 Make up the rolls: lay strips of eggplant on a board, then sprinkle them with Parmesan cheese and season with black pepper. Cover each eggplant strip with a zucchini strip, then form them into loose rolls. Pack them into an ovenproof dish.

3 Bake in the oven for 15–20 minutes or until the rolls are cooked through. Season to taste and sprinkle with the hemp seeds. Garnish with parsley sprigs and serve from the baking dish.

HEMP FLOUR CHOCOLATE BROWNIES

½ cup organic hemp flour

2 fresh eggs, beaten

1 tbsp vanilla extract

1 tsp salt

1 tbs hemp seeds

9 dates, pitted and finely chopped

3 tbsp molasses

3 tbsp canola oil

½ cup almond butter

½ cup cocoa powder

½ cup dark chocolate chips

1 tsp baking power

Serves 4–6

1 Place all the ingredients in a food processor and blend.

2 Grease and line a small square pan, then add the mixture and bake at 325ºF for 20–25 minutes. Allow to cool, then cut into squares before removing from the pan.

CARAWAY SEED

Botanical name: *Carum carvi*
Family: *Apiaceae*

Caraway, sometimes referred to as wild cumin, Persian cumin or meridian fennel, is a biennial plant in the Apiaceae family, native to Asia, North Africa and Europe; it can be grown as an annual in more temperate climates. The leaves are feathery, like those of the carrot, and it is also related to dill, anise, fennel and cumin. The flowers are small and can be pink or white. The fruits, erroneously referred to as seeds, which are in fact crescent-shaped achenes with five pale ridges, have a sweet, anise-like flavor.

The plant prefers sunny locations and well-drained, rich soil. The fruits/seeds are harvested early on in the day by cutting the plant stalks down;

these are threshed, once dried, thereby shedding the seeds. Being dried, caraway is available all year round, either as whole seeds or ground into a powder. They should be sealed in containers and stored in a cool, dry place, but not for long. Caraway is used to flavor bread, and is added to savory dishes, such as sauerkraut, goulash, curries, and liqueurs.

Health benefits: Caraway has a long tradition of medicinal use, primarily for stomach complaints, and there is evidence to suggest that it can be used as an endocrine function support agent, specifically related to thyroid disorders and autoimmune diseases. Caraway is good for heartburn, bloating, flatulence, gastrointestinal spasms and for menstrual cramps. It is also an antioxidant and contains vitamins A, B-complex, C, E, iron, copper, calcium, potassium, manganese, selenium, zinc and magnesium.

CARAWAY CAKE

½ cup softened butter
¾ cup white sugar
1 egg, beaten
2½ cups all-purpose flour
1 tsp baking soda
1 tsp baking powder
½ cup milk
1 tbsp caraway seeds

Serves 8–10

1 Preheat the oven to 350° F. Grease and line a medium loaf pan.

2 In a mixing bowl, cream together the butter and sugar, then slowly add the beaten egg. Gradually fold in the flour, baking soda and baking powder, then add the milk and mix well.

3 Pour the mixture into the prepared loaf pan, adding a sprinkling of caraway seeds to the top.

4 Bake for about 45 minutes or until a skewer, inserted into the center, comes out clean. Leave the cake to cool in the pan before turning it out.

FRESH SAUERKRAUT SALAD

1 tbsp olive oil
1 medium red onion, thinly sliced
2 sticks celery, finely chopped
1 medium white cabbage, finely
 shredded, tough veins removed
1¼ cups cider vinegar
½ cup apple cider
1 tsp caraway seeds
½ cup water
1 tbsp salt
Chopped scallions to garnish

1 Heat the oil in a large pot set over a medium heat. Sauté the onion and celery, stirring constantly, until they are soft and translucent.

2 Add the cabbage, vinegar, cider, caraway seeds, water and salt and bring to a boil.

3 Cover and simmer for 30–45 minutes until the cabbage is tender (adding more water, if necessary, to stop the mixture from drying out).

4 Store the sauerkraut salad in a covered container in a refrigerator and consume within 2 days.

CORIANDER SEED

Botanical name: *Coriandrum sativum*
Family: *Apiaceae*

Coriander, also known as Chinese or Mexican parsley or dhania, in the Indian subcontinent, is an annual herb (leaves) and spice (seeds) in the Apiaceae family and is related to the carrot. Cilantro, not to be confused with culanto (*Eryngium foetidum*), which is a

close relative, is the Spanish for coriander, but is the word commonly used for coriander leaves in North America due to the influence of Mexican cuisine.

Coriander is native to a large part of southern Europe, North Africa and Asia. The leaves taste differently from the seeds, which have pleasant citrus overtones, and indeed the Chinese believed that coriander seeds had the power to bestow immortality. The leaves, however, are something of an acquired taste, the flavor having been compared to the smell emitted by stink bugs, in which similar chemical groups are involved (aldehydes). Once converted, however, its fans would be loath to do without it.

Coriander seeds, like many spices, contain antioxidants which can delay or prevent spoilage of food, while both the leaves and the seeds have been found to contain antioxidant and antibacterial properties, although the leaves exerted a stronger effect. Coriander has been used as a folk medicine for the relief of anxiety and insomnia, and in traditional Indian medicine as a

diuretic by boiling equal amounts of coriander and cumin seeds, then cooling them and consuming the resulting liquid. In holistic medicine, coriander is used to relieve flatulence and as an effective aid to digestion.

Health benefits: Coriander has antibacterial and anti-inflammatory properties and is useful in the treatment of urinary tract infections, nausea and digestive problems; it freshens the breath, reduces blood sugar levels and is thought to lower (bad) cholesterol. Coriander seeds contain many vitamins, including A, K and C. They are also a good source of folic acid, magnesium and calcium.

SPICY PUMPKIN SOUP

2 tbsp olive oil
½ tsp ground coriander seeds
½ tsp ground fennel seeds
1 large onion, chopped
1 tsp minced fresh ginger
2 cloves garlic, minced
1¼ pts vegetable stock
2 lbs fresh pumpkin, peeled and
  with the seeds removed and the
  flesh cut into chunks
2 tbsp freshly squeezed lime juice
⅓ pt coconut milk
Salt and pepper to taste
Fresh coriander (cilantro) leaves
  and sliced red chilis to garnish

Serves 4

1 In a large pot, heat the olive oil and gently fry the ground coriander and fennel seeds for approximately one minute.

2 Add the onion, ginger and garlic, and gently cook for a further three to four minutes.

3 Add the stock, pumpkin and lime juice and simmer gently until the pumpkin is almost soft.

4 Add the coconut milk and continue to cook very gently until the pumpkin is totally cooked. Using a stick blender, process until a smooth soup is achieved. Serve garnished with the chopped coriander (cilantro) leaves and chili.

VEGETABLE SAMOSAS

FOR THE FILLING:
4 large potatoes
3 tbsp vegetable oil
1 tsp crushed cumin seeds
1 tsp crushed coriander seeds
2 green chilies, finely chopped
3 cloves garlic, minced
5 oz frozen peas
Salt
2 tsp garam masala paste
½ tsp chili powder
1 tbsp lemon juice
Handful fresh coriander (cilantro)
 leaves, chopped
Oil for deep frying

FOR THE PASTRY:
8 oz plain flour
½ tsp salt
4 tbsp cooking oil
Water

Makes 16 samosas

MAKE THE FILLING:
1 Parboil the potatoes in water for
10 minutes. Drain, cool and chop
them into very small cubes.

2 In a skillet, heat the oil and
lightly fry the crushed cumin and
coriander seeds. Add the chilies

and garlic and cook for a minute
or so longer.

3 Add the potatoes, peas, salt,
garam masala, chili powder and
lemon juice. Stir until everything
in the skillet is combined. Cook
over a low heat for 5–6 minutes,
stirring gently. Check seasoning
and add the chopped coriander
(cilantro) leaves. Leave the filling
to cool.

MAKE THE PASTRY:
1 In a bowl, and using your
fingers, rub the flour, salt and oil
together until the mixture
resembles breadcrumbs.

2. Adding a little water at a time,
knead the dough on a floured
surface until smooth and roll into
a ball. Cover in plastic wrap and
set aside at room temperature for
30 minutes.

MAKE THE SAMOSAS:
1 Make a little 'glue' by adding
2–3 tbsp of water to 1 tbsp plain
flour and mixing it to a thick
paste. Set aside.

2 With oiled hands, divide the
dough into 8–9 portions and roll

them into balls. As you make
them, keep them covered with a
damp cloth to prevent them from
drying out.

3 On a lightly greased surface, roll
out one ball at a time to form a
7–8-inch circle approximately ⅛
inch thick. With a knife, cut each
into half to form two half circles.

4 Place a little glue along the flat
edge of each half circle and fold in
half to form a cone. Fill with the
potato mixture, leaving enough

space to close it. Add more glue along the opening and seal, making sure there are no gaps. Gently crimp the edges. Repeat until all the samosas have been made, keeping them under a damp cloth to prevent them from drying out.

5 Using a wok or deep-sided skillet, add sufficient oil to more than cover a samosa. Bring to a medium heat, testing to see that the oil is not too hot by placing a small piece of dough into the oil, which should sizzle gently and rise to the top.

6 Place a few samosas at a time in the wok, being careful not to overcrowd, and fry gently, turning them from time to time until golden brown. Remove and drain on kitchen paper. Repeat until all the samosas have been cooked. Serve hot with chutney.

PUMPKIN SEED

Botanical name: *Cucurbita pepo*
Family: *Cucurbitaceae*

The pumpkin is an herbaceous running plant belonging to the melon family, which grows annually on vines that may reach up to 26 ft in length. It has large, bristly leaves and bears large, yellow flowers from which the fruit will eventually develop.

Although pumpkins are usually orange or yellow, other colors such as green, white, red and gray are also possible. It is not known for sure where pumpkins came from, although they are thought to have originated in North America, the oldest evidence being the discovery of pumpkin seeds, dating from between 7000 and 5500 BC, found in Mexico. Pumpkin pie is still traditionally eaten during Thanksgiving in America, and pumpkins are also hollowed out around Halloween, when they are filled with candles and set in windows to deter evil spirits.

North American tribes were the very first to discover the health benefits of pumpkin seeds, which were an important part of their diet and were also used for medicinal purposes. They referred to them as 'cucurbita' and used them to treat kidney problems and to elimate intestinal parasites.

Today, pumpkin seeds are a feature of many cuisines and cultures. Roasted seeds can be added to soups and salads to provide a nutty flavor or they are commonly eaten as snacks.

Health benefits: Pumpkins seeds are a natural source of useful constituents such as carbohydrates, amino acids and unsaturated fatty acids. They contain B-complex vitamins, also vitamins C, D, E and K, and are loaded with other nutrients such as calcium, potassium and phosphorus. They are said to be of benefit to those with bladder problems, and are good for mental and cardiovascular health.

PUMPKIN SEED & GOJI BERRY GRANOLA

¼ cup brown sugar
¼ cup honey
2 tbsp vegetable oil
½ tsp salt
1½ cups rolled oats
½ cup roughly chopped almonds
½ cup raw pumpkin seeds
⅓ cup dried goji berries or
 cranberries

Serves 3-4

1 Preheat the oven to 300°F. Place the brown sugar, honey, vegetable oil and salt in a large mixing bowl and stir until all the ingredients are well-combined. Add the rest of the ingredients, apart from the berries, and stir thoroughly until everything is completely coated in the sugar-honey mixture.

2 Pour the mixture onto a sheet pan lined with baking parchment, or use a non-stick cookie sheet. Spread evenly, and leave the ingredients to toast in the oven for 15 minutes.

3 Remove the granola from the oven and break it up with a fork. Spread the mixture out again and return it to the oven for another 15 minutes or until the mixture develops a good crunch.

4 Remove from the oven and leave to cool at room temperature. Add the dried berries and serve with milk or yogurt.

CARDAMOM

Botanical name: *Elattaria cardamomum*
Family: *Zingiberaceae*

Cardamon, both green and black, are plants belonging to the ginger family, *Zingiberaceae*. Cardamom, often called the 'queen of spices' is native to India, Nepal and Bhutan, where its use dates back some 5000 years and where in some areas it still grows wild. Today, it is also grown in some South American countries, with Guatemala in Central America being the largest producer.

The green cardamom is a perennial that grows in thick clumps and which starts to produce its prized seed pods after two years. Traditionally, the pods are crushed to extract the highly aromatic seeds that are used in both food and drink and for medicinal

purposes. Cardamom is a common ingredient in Indian, Scandinavian and Middle Eastern cooking, and lends itself particularly well to sweet, milky puddings, cakes and chutneys. The seeds are also used to impart a unique flavor to tea and coffee. Black cardamom has a distinctly more smoky, though not bitter, aroma, with a pleasant coolness reminiscent of mint.

Cardamom confers many health benefits when consumed and its essential oils are also used in aromatherapy. The spicy pods contain many essential oils.

Health benefits: Used to treat coughs, colds, sore throats, chest infections, heartburn, gastrointestinal problems, flatulence, gall bladder problems and urinary infections. Contains vitamins A, B-complex, C, iron, zinc, phosphorous, manganese, potassium and useful antioxidants.

CHICKEN CURRY

3 tbsp vegetable oil
1 small onion, chopped
2 cloves garlic, minced
2 tsp garam masala
2 tsp turmeric
1 tsp cardamom powder, or 8-10
 pods, crushed
1 tsp ground cinnamon
1 tsp paprika
1 bay leaf
½ tsp grated fresh ginger
½ teaspoon white sugar
Salt to taste
4 skinless, boneless chicken
 breasts, cubed
1 tbsp tomato paste
1 cup plain yogurt
½ lemon, juiced
½ teaspoon cayenne pepper

Serves 4–6

1 Heat the oil in a skillet over a medium heat. Sauté the onion until lightly browned, then stir in the garlic, garam masala, turmeric, cardamom, cinnamon, paprika, bay leaf, ginger, sugar and salt. Continue stirring for 2 minutes.

2 Add the chicken pieces and stir until they become well-coated in the spices.

3 Add the tomato paste and yogurt, then bring to a boil, reduce the heat, and simmer for 20 to 25 minutes.

4 Remove the bay leaf, and stir in the lemon juice and cayenne pepper. Simmer for a further 5 minutes or so before serving.

CARDAMOM ICE CREAM (KULFI)

1 slice white bread
4 cups whole milk
1 tsp cornstarch
½ cup sugar
½ tsp ground cardamom seeds
Pistachios

Serves 6

1 Remove the crust from the bread and break it into small pieces. Place the bread in a small bowl, add ½ cup milk and the cornstarch, and mix thoroughly to create a smooth paste. Set aside.

2 In a non-stick pot, bring the remaining milk slowly to a boil, stirring constantly to prevent sticking or burning. Continue boiling the milk until it is reduced to approximately 2½ cups.

3 Add the bread mixture to the milk and cook for another 4 minutes, reducing the heat to a simmer. Add the sugar and cardamom and cook for 2 more minutes.

4 Pour the milk mixture into a container and leave to cool to room temperature.

5 When completely cooled, cover the milk with plastic wrap, making sure it rests on the surface of the milk.

6 Put the container into the freezer, allowing 7 hours for it to freeze. Serve the kulfi in bowls garnished with chopped pistachios.

SUNFLOWER SEED

Botanical name: *Helianthus annuus*
Family: *Asteraceae*

The sunflower or helianthus (in Greek, *helios* means sun and *anthos* flower) is a plant indigenous to the Americas, having been domesticated nearly 3000 years ago by Native Americans before being brought to Europe and elsewhere.

The sunflower has a large inflorescence (flowering head), a rough, hairy stem, broad, coarsely-toothed, rough leaves and a circular flower head. The heads, which in their bud stage follow the position of the sun, consist of many individual flowers which mature into seeds, often in their hundreds, on a receptacle base. The leaves of the sunflower

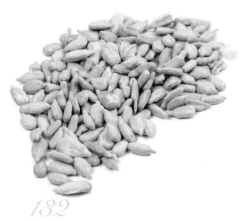

can be used as cattle feed, while the stems contain a fiber used in paper production.

Today, sunflowers are mainly cultivated for their seeds and the valuable oil that is extracted from them, which is widely used in cooking. The seeds themselves are most nutritious and can be eaten as a snack or added to meals for additional flavor and texture. They are known for their high levels of vitamin E in particular, but are loaded with many other nutrients that are essential to a healthy life.

Health benefits: Sunflower seeds have many beneficial constituents including B-complex vitamins, vitamin E, calcium, selenium, zinc, phosphorus, magnesium, volatile essential oils, tannin, proteins, phyosterols (plant fats) and antioxidants. They are useful as an anti-cancer treatment, good for arthritis, constipation, lowering (bad) cholesterol and may be helpful in treating multiple sclerosis.

SUNFLOWER SEED & HONEY BREAD

2 packages (¼ oz each) active dry
 yeast
3¼ cups warm water (110°F)
¼ cup white bread flour
⅓ cup canola oil
⅓ cup runny honey
3 tsp salt

6½ cups whole wheat flour
½ cup sunflower seeds
3 tbsp melted butter

Makes 3 loaves

1 In a large bowl, dissolve the yeast in the warm water and set aside until activated. Then add the bread flour, oil, honey, salt and 4 cups of the whole wheat flour. Mix together until smooth.

2 Stir in the sunflower seeds and enough of the remaining flour to form a firm dough.

3 Turn the dough onto a floured surface, then knead until smooth and elastic (about 8 minutes). Place the ball of dough in a lightly oiled bowl, turning once to oil the top. Cover and leave to rise in a warm place until doubled in size (about 1 hour).

4 Punch the dough down in the bowl, then remove and divide it into three equal portions. Shape into loaves and put into three greased 8 x 4-inch loaf pans. Cover and leave to rise again for about 30 minutes.

5 Pre-heat the oven to 350°F. Brush the tops of the loaves with melted butter and bake for 35–40 minutes or until the loaves are golden brown. (A skewer should come out clean and dry if the bread is done). Remove from the pans to wire racks to cool.

SUNFLOWER SEED COOKIES

1 cup white sugar
1 cup soft light-brown sugar
1 cup softened butter
2 eggs
1 tsp vanilla extract
5 cups all-purpose flour
½ tsp baking powder
1 tsp baking soda
1 cup sunflower seeds

Makes approx 25–35 cookies

1 Preheat the oven to 350°F. In a large bowl, cream together the white sugar, brown sugar and softened butter until pale and fluffy. Beat in the eggs, one at a time, then stir in the vanilla extract.

2 Add the flour, baking powder and baking soda, mixing them into the creamed mixture until well-blended.

3 Using ungreased cookie sheets. drop teaspoonfuls of the dough onto the sheets, leaving enough room for each to spread out.

Cover each cookie with sunflower seeds.

4 Bake for 10–12 minutes or until the cookies begin to brown around the edges. Allow the cookies to cool and harden for a few minutes before transferring them to wire racks to cool completely.

FLAXSEED

Botanical name: *Linum usitatissimum*
Family: *Linaceae*

Common flaxseed is also known as linseed. It is a food and fiber crop that is grown in cooler regions of the world. The earliest evidence of human use of the wild form of flax has been discovered in the present-day Republic of Georgia, where spun and knotted flax fibers were found in the Dzudzuana Caves dating back 30,000 years.

There are two common cultivars of flax; one is predominantly grown for its oil and seeds and the other for its fiber. Flax was extensively cultivated in ancient Egypt, where the plant was depicted on wall paintings, and it

was also grown by the Romans, its use eventually spreading throughout the Mediterranean.

Today, flax is grown principally for its oil, used mainly to treat wooden furniture, and for its fibers which are made into linen cloth. As a food source, flaxseeds are now considered to be a 'superfood,' and a variety of important health benefits have subsequently been claimed.

Flaxseeds are readily available from grocery and health food stores. They can be added to baked goods, stews, breakfast cereals, pancakes, smoothies and yogurts to which they impart a nutty, wholesome flavor that is reminiscent of wheat germ.

Health benefits: As with other oilseeds, flaxseeds are very high in calories but low in saturated fat. They are an excellent source of numerous health-giving nutrients, being rich in dietary fiber and antioxidants. They are claimed to be able to lower (bad) cholesterol and have anti-inflammatory properties. They lower the risk of high blood pressure and can help prevent some cancers. Flaxseeds are rich in vitamin E, folates and other B-complex vitamins, together with manganese, potassium, calcium, iron, magnesium, zinc and selenium.

KALE, APPLE, FLAXSEED & KIWI SMOOTHIE

3 cups pure apple juice
¾ cup chopped kale leaves (ribs and stems removed)
2 kiwi fruits, peeled and sliced
1 tsp crushed flaxseeds
3 tsp runny honey
¾ cup ice cubes
Juice of 1 lime

Serves 2

Put all the ingredients into a blender and process until smooth.

POPPY SEED

Botanical name: *Papaver somniferum*
Family: *Papaveraceae*

Poppy seeds are oilseeds obtained from *Papaver somniferum,* the sleep-inducing poppy, the seed pod of which is the principal source of most naturally occurring opioids. Incisions are made on the green seed pods, causing latex to ooze, which is collected and dried to produce raw opium, a process which, in many countries, is either illegal or requires special permits.

The seeds themselves, which are tiny, contain very small amounts of opiates, and have no measurable narcotic effect when used in small quantities. The seeds are used whole or they can be ground or pressed to make poppy seed oil.

Poppy seeds are blue-gray or ivory in color, the former being more common in European cookery, the latter in Indian cuisine. They are widely used as a spice and decoration in baked goods, such as muffins, bagels and cakes. The seeds of *Papaver somniferum* have a mild, nutty taste. Today, their cultivation is a commercial enterprise in many countries, including Turkey, France, India and parts of Eastern Europe.

Poppy seeds are also used in animal feeds and are often added to birdseed formulae, while the oil is used in cooking and soap-making. In some cultures, poppy seeds are seen as a symbol of virility and they have also been used historically in divination.

Health benefits: Poppy seeds are a good source of carbohydrates and calcium, while the oil, which contains linoleic acid, is known to protect the body against cardiovascular disease and heart attack. The seeds are also a source of oleic acid, which is believed to guard against some cancers and contain minerals such as iron, copper, calcium, potassium, manganese, zinc and magnesium.

POPPY SEED ROLL

½ lb poppy seeds
¾ cup white sugar
1 tbsp melted butter
1 tbsp lemon juice
½ cup hot milk
1 (¼ oz) package active dry yeast
½ cup warm water (100°F)
2 tbsp white sugar
2 cups all-purpose flour (slightly
 more, if needed)
½ tsp salt
¼ cup butter
1 egg, separated into yolk and
 white
Makes 2 rolls

1 Put the poppy seeds into a food processor and grind them up. (Alternatively, the seeds may be ground by hand using a pestle and mortar.) Put the ground poppy seeds into a bowl with the ¼ cup of sugar, 1 tbsp melted butter, the lemon juice and hot milk, stir thoroughly, cover, and place in the refrigerator (the filling will gradually start to thicken).

2 Mix the yeast with the warm water and the 2 tablespoonfuls of sugar in a small bowl. Set aside until the yeast becomes active.

3 Place the flour and salt in a large bowl, then rub the ¼ cup butter into the flour mixture until it resembles coarse crumbs. Pour the yeast and the egg yolk into the flour mixture and stir to make a soft dough.

4 Turn the dough out onto a floured work surface and knead until smooth and slightly springy. (If the dough seems too sticky, knead in more flour, a little at a time.)

5 Cut the dough in half and roll each piece out into a 12 x 16-inch rectangle. Spread half the poppy seed filling over each rectangle, leaving a 1-inch border. Roll up each rectangle from the long end like a jelly roll. Pinch the seams together to secure.

6 Place the rolls, seam sides down, on a sheet pan lined with baking parchment. Set aside in a warm place to rise for about an hour.

7 Preheat the oven to 350°F. Beat the egg white in a bowl until frothy, then use it to brush over the surfaces of the rolls. Bake the rolls in the oven until they are a dark golden brown (30–40 minutes). Remove from the oven and cover the rolls with a clean cloth until cool (this will keep the crusts soft). Allow to cool completely before slicing.

LEMON & POPPY SEED MUFFINS

2 cups unbleached all-purpose
 flour
2 tsp baking powder
¼ tsp salt
½ cup softened unsalted butter
1 tsp finely grated lemon zest
⅔ cup granulated sugar
2 large eggs
4 tsp poppy seeds
½ cup milk

Makes 12 muffins

1 Preheat the oven to 375°F. Place paper muffin cases in a 12-cup muffin pan and set it aside.

2 Sift the flour, baking powder and salt into a medium bowl and set aside.

3 In a large mixing bowl, cream together the butter, lemon zest and sugar until light and fluffy. Add the eggs, one at a time, beating well after each addition and making sure that all the ingredients are thoroughly mixed. Stir in the poppy seeds.

4 Fold the flour mixture, a third at a time, into the butter mixture, alternating each third with half the milk, until just combined. (Take care not to overmix the batter.) Divide the batter between the muffin cups and bake until golden brown (about 25 minutes). Let the muffins cool before serving.

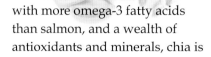

CHIA SEED
Botanical name: *Salvia hispanica*
Family: *Lamiaceae*

Chia is a species of flowering plant belonging to the mint family, *Lamiaceae*, native to central and southern Guatemala and Mexico. The plant can sprout in a matter of days, but its appeal lies in the nutritive punch packed by its tiny seeds.

The word *chia* derives from the Nahuati word meaning oily, and with more omega-3 fatty acids than salmon, and a wealth of antioxidants and minerals, chia is a complete source of protein. There is evidence that it was first cultivated by the Aztecs in pre-

Columbian times, when it was regarded as an important food crop. Nowadays, the seeds are used ground or whole and are commonly added to the food and drinks of many Central and South American countries.

During the last 30 years or so, chia seeds have come to be part of a health-food craze which has spread throughout North America and Western Europe. The seeds are fairly bland in taste, with a slight nutty flavor, and they are typically added to breads, sweets, snacks, yogurts and seasonings. Chia seeds, however, have the unique property of swelling up when mixed with water, making a thick gel, rather like tapioca in texture, which is often made into a health drink.

Health benefits: Chia seeds contain calcium, manganese, phosphorus, omega-3 fatty acids and fiber. Good for combating diabetes and helpful for those trying to lose weight, they are credited with regulating the appetite, improving heart function and maintaining healthy cholesterol levels.

CHIA PUDDING WITH COCONUT & STRAWBERRIES

2½ cups milk
5 tbsp chia seeds
4 tbsp desiccated coconut
1 tsp vanilla extract
Fresh strawberries, halved

Serves 2

1 Mix the milk, chia seeds, desiccated coconut and vanilla extract together in a bowl and stir well.

2 Allow the mixture to stand for ten minutes, stirring occasionally.

3 Refrigerate overnight. Stir well before serving and top with the fresh strawberries.

CHIA BREAKFAST

3 cups natural yogurt, chilled
1 tsp runny honey
2 tbsp chia seeds
1½ cups granola
Fresh berries
Pomegranate seeds

Serves 2

1 In a medium-sized bowl, mix the yogurt with the honey.

2 In two large serving glasses, divide a quarter of the yogurt between the two glasses. Add the chia seeds and mix well.

3 Next add the granola, dividing it equally between the two glasses.

4 Finally, top the glasses up with the remaining yogurt and garnish with mixed berries and chia and pomegranate seeds.

SESAME SEED

Botanical name: *Sesamum indicum*
Family: *Pedaliaceae*

Sesame is a flowering plant in the *Pedaliaceae* family, with numerous wild relatives occurring in Africa and with a lesser number in India. It was first domesticated around 4,000 years ago when it was widely cultivated throughout the Middle East.

Sesame was known to the Babylonians and Assyrians, and the ancient Egyptians called it *sesemt*, including it in the list of medicinal drugs in the Ebers Papryus, believed to be over 3,600 years old.

Today, the plant has become naturalized in many tropical regions of the world, where it is cultivated for its edible seeds.

The sesame plant is generally grown as an oilseed crop, valued as having one of the highest oil contents of any seed.

Seasame oil has a distinctive, nutty flavor and is a common ingredient of many cuisines worldwide. Sesame seeds come in many colors, depending on the cultivar, the most common variety being off-white, although buff, tan, gold, brown, reddish, gray and black varieties are not uncommon. A sesame crop can also be grown in harsh, drought-like conditions where other crops would struggle to survive, even though it favors well-drained sandy soil and a warm environment to flourish.

Sesame is grown extensively in Burma, China and India, and is also an important commercial crop in Africa, Nigeria, Sudan and Ethiopia in particular.

Health benefits: Sesame is an important source of phytonutrients such as fatty acids, flavonoid phenolic antioxidants, vitamins and dietary fiber. It is credited with lowering (bad) cholesterol, preventing stroke, heart problems, cancer and respiratory problems. It reduces high blood pressure and is good for bone health.

HONEY-GLAZED SALMON WITH SESAME SEEDS

2 salmon fillets
2 tsp runny honey
1 tsp light soy sauce
1 tsp white sesame seeds
1 tsp black sesame seeds

Serves 2

1 Preheat the oven to 375ºF.

2 Place the salmon fillets on an oiled sheet pan.

3 Mix the honey and soy sauce together in a small bowl and coat each fillet evenly with the mixture.

4 Mix the sesame seeds together and sprinkle them over the tops of the fillets. Place in the oven for 20 minutes or until the salmon is cooked through and the top has started to caramelize slightly. Serve on a bed of rice accompanied by lemon wedges.

LEGUMES
&
PULSES

CHAPTER THREE

LEGUMES & PULSES

CHICKPEA
Botanical name: *Cicer arietinum*
Family: *Fabaceae*

The chickpea is a legume in the
Fabaceae family also known as the
Bengal gram, garbanzo bean and
Egyptian pea. It was one of the
earliest legumes to be cultivated,
its use in the Middle East dating
back 7,500 years. Its cultivation
has also been documented in
ancient Greece and Rome, where it
was regarded as a staple food. The
Latin name for chickpea, *Cicer
arietinum*, means 'small ram,'
reflecting the unique shape of the
chickpea that is said to resemble a
ram's head.

There are three main cultivars of
chickpea; *Desi*, which is smaller
and darker and mostly cultivated

in India; 'Bombay,' which is also dark but slightly larger in size, and *Kabuli* (associated with Kabul in Afghanistan), which is somewhat lighter and smoother in texture than the other two.

Chickpeas have a delicious nutty, buttery taste, and when mature can be eaten in salads, cooked in stews, or made into gram flour (also known as chickpea flour). Hummus is a famous Arabic and Mediterranean dish made from chickpeas and, in fact, *hummus* is the Arabic word for chickpea. The ingredients used to make hummus include chickpeas, olive oil and tahini or sesame paste.

Health benefits: The nutritional constituents of chickpeas include unique antioxidants such as vitamins C, E, beta-carotene and phytonutrients. The consumption of chickpeas is of benefit to the digestive tract, decreases the risk of cardiovascular disease, regulates blood sugars, and reduces (bad) cholesterol. Chickpeas increase satiety and therefore serve to lessen calorific intake for those trying to maintain weight-loss diets.

CHICKPEA & TOMATO SALSA

1 red onion, finely chopped
1 clove garlic, minced
½ tsp chili powder
3 tbsp extra virgin olive oil
4 fresh tomatoes, quartered
½ cup roughly-chopped sundried tomatoes
15 oz chopped canned tomatoes
1 tsp finely chopped coriander (cilantro) leaves
15 oz canned chickpeas, rinsed and drained
Salt and pepper to taste
Fresh herbs to garnish

Serves 4–6

1 In a large pot, gently sauté the onion, garlic and chili powder in the olive oil. When the onions are soft, add ALL the tomatoes, the coriander and the chickpeas.

2 Leave to simmer for about 30 minutes, stirring occasionally, until the mixture thickens.

3 Season well and serve hot or cold on toasted croutons garnished with fresh herbs.

CHICKPEA & COUSCOUS SALAD

8 oz couscous
5 tbsp olive oil
Zest and juice of 1 lemon
1 tbsp white wine vinegar
1 tbsp runny honey
Salt and pepper to taste
15 oz canned chickpeas, rinsed
 and drained
1 cup fresh pomegranate seeds
½ cup flaked almonds
2 tbsp finely chopped fresh mint

Serves 4–6

1 Prepare the couscous according to the package instructions. While still warm, mix in 1 tbsp of the olive oil, salt, and leave to cool.

2 Make the dressing by combining the zest and juice of the lemon, vinegar, honey and the rest of the olive oil. Season well with salt and pepper.

3 Give the couscous a mix and pour it into a large bowl. Add the dressing and mix again.

4 Add the chickpeas, pomegranate seeds and almonds and mix together. Check seasoning then sprinkle in the fresh mint to serve.

SOY BEAN

Botanical name: *Glycine max*
Family: *Fabaceae*

Known as the soybean in the United States and soya bean in the UK, *Glycine max* is a species of legume native to East Asia. In China it is known as 'large bean,' and in Japan as 'yellow bean,' the immature bean also bearing the name of 'edamame bean.' The plant was first domesticated in the eastern half of northern China in around the 11th century BC. Grown mainly for its seeds, it quickly became established as an indispensible part of the Asian diet, where a large variety of fresh, fermented and dried food products were already consumed.

Today, soy is grown all over the world for a number of purposes, including animal feed, flour, meal, soy milk, soy vegetable oil, and other products such as tofu, tempeh, soy sauce, etc. The United States is one of the world's major producers and exporters of soy, where most of the crop is processed into oil for a number of purposes as well as for meal destined mainly for animal feed.

benefits, with soy protein being a source of phytochemicals and many other important nutrients. It is a rich repository of calcium and helps reduce the risk of osteoporosis by increasing bone density. It is also known to ease menopausal symptoms and help regulate estrogen levels. It is good for heart health and is also claimed to prevent cancer.

Soy by-products, such as tofu, tempeh and soy milk, contain all the essential amino acids which combine well with those of cereals, such as wheat, rice and corn, making them of particular value in the vegan diet.

The oil is made into shortening, margarine and cooking oils, and is also used in paint, varnishes, caulking compounds, printing inks and other products.

As a food source, most people associate soy with meat or dairy substitutes and while this is often the case, soy has many additional food uses, which include the addition of soy proteins to baby formulae, sport and weight-reducing drinks.

Health benefits: There is no denying that soy has many health

TOFU & VEGETABLES IN OYSTER SAUCE

8 mushrooms
1 tsp soy sauce
1 tsp superfine sugar
1 tsp sesame oil
1 tbsp water
3 tbsp oyster sauce
1 tsp sugar
2 tsp sesame oil
1 cup firm, sliced tofu
A little cornstarch
2 tbsp oil
1 tbsp finely minced garlic
1 medium onion, chopped
Pinch of salt
Assorted vegetables (broccoli florets, sliced snow peas, baby sweetcorn, etc.

Serves 2–3

1 Slice the mushrooms and marinate them in the soy sauce, sugar and 1 tsp sesame oil for 20 minutes. Meanwhile, make the sauce by mixing together the water, oyster sauce, sugar and 2 tsp sesame oil. Set aside.

2 Pat dry the tofu slices, dredge them in cornstarch and set them aside. Heat a large wok with 1 tbsp oil over a high heat. Reduce the heat, then stir-fry the tofu until evenly brown on all sides. Transfe to a warm serving dish.

3 In the same wok, heat the other tbsp oil over a high heat and brie stir-fry the garlic, browning it ver slightly. Stir in the onion and salt, and continue to cook until soft.

4 Add the mushrooms and their marinade together with the rest o the vegetables and stir-fry. Stir in the sauce and heat through. Pour the sauce and vegetables over the reserved tofu and serve.

SUPERFOOD SALAD WITH GINGER MISO DRESSING

¼ cup grapeseed or peanut oil
¼ cup rice vinegar
3 tbsp sweet white or yellow miso
1 tbsp dark sesame oil
1 tbsp fresh minced ginger
1 clove garlic, minced
A pinch chili powder
2 tsp runny honey
2 large handfuls baby spinach
1 cup shredded carrot
8 grape tomatoes, left whole
1½ cups shelled edamame soy beans
½ 15-oz can chickpeas, rinsed and drained
½ cup dried cranberries
½ cup cooked quinoa

Serves 2

1 Make the dressing by adding the oil, vinegar, miso, sesame oil, ginger, garlic, chili powder and honey to a small blender and processing them until smooth.

2 In 2 bowls, build the salad, starting with the spinach, carrot and tomatoes. Top with the edamame beans, chickpeas, cranberries and quinoa. Spoon the dressing over the salad and serve.

LENTIL

Botanical name: *Lens culinaris*
Family: *Fabaceae*

The lentil is an edible pulse belonging to the legume family, the seeds of which grow in pods, usually with two seeds in each. Lentils are related to beans and peanuts and are similar in appearance to dried split peas, although less sweet in taste. It is believed that lentils originated in the Near East where they were first domesticated. Lentils have been part of the human diet since

Neolithic times and there is archeological evidence to show that they were consumed between 9,500 and 13,000 years ago. References to lentils may be found in the Hebrew Bible and in Egyptian tombs.

It is interesting to note that the modern-day 'lens' is named after the lentil, due to the similarity in their shapes. Lentils are relatively easy to cultivate, in that they are tolerant of drought, making them suitable for cultivation in more arid parts of the world. Today the main producers are Canada, India, Turkey and Australia.

Lentils are a very versatile ingredient. They make a hearty addition to soups and stews and are a main ingredient of the Indian *dal*. In the Middle East, lentils are added to a number of different dishes, such as the popular *mejadra*, which also includes rice and fried onions.

Lentils do not have a very strong flavor of their own, so they are used to give texture and nutritive substance to spicy dishes. There are three main types of lentils, the most common being the brown lentil, while the small, dark-green lentils, known as Puy or French lentils, are valued for their high quality and taste. Lastly, there are the red lentils, where the hulls have been removed and the seeds split like split peas.

Health benefits: Lentils are rich in carbohydrates and protein but virtually fat-free. They are very high in fiber, which is said to substantially reduce the risk of developing heart disease. Other benefits are numerous, such as the balancing of blood sugar levels, the replenishment of the body's iron stores, and the fact that they are a source of slow-burning energy. They are of benefit to the digestive, nervous and immune systems and are valuable in lowering (bad) cholesterol.

CREAM OF LENTIL SOUP

6 cups chicken or vegetable stock
2 cups dried red lentils, rinsed
1 bay leaf
1 medium onion, chopped
2 celery sticks, chopped
2 cloves garlic, minced
2 tbsp butter
2 medium carrots, chopped
1 tsp sugar
½ tsp curry powder
Salt and freshly ground black
 pepper
1½ cups heavy cream
1 tbsp lemon juice

Serves 6–8

1 To a large pot, add the stock, lentils and bay leaf. Bring to a boil, then reduce the heat, cover, and simmer for 25–30 minutes or until the lentils are tender.

2 In another large pot, sauté the onion, celery and garlic in the butter until tender but not browned. Add the carrots, sugar, curry powder, salt and pepper, and sauté until all the vegetables are tender.

3 Remove the bay leaf and add the lentils and stock to the vegetable mixture. Return to a boil and leave to simmer for another 5 minutes.

4 Using a stick blender in the same pot, process the soup until smooth, then stir in the cream and lemon juice.

5 Return the soup to the heat and reheat thoroughly but gently, without boiling. Check the seasoning and serve.

DAL

1 cup yellow or brown lentils
2 tbsp vegetable oil
1 tsp mustard seeds
3 onions, chopped
2 tbsp fresh minced ginger
6 cloves garlic, minced
1 tsp ground coriander seeds
1 tsp ground cumin
1 tsp salt
1 cup water
Fresh coriander (cilantro) to
 garnish

Serves 6

1 Boil the lentils in water until
tender. Drain and set aside.

2 Heat the oil and add the
mustard seeds, frying them for
about ½ minute. Add the onions,
ginger and garlic and sauté them
until the onions turn golden
brown. Add the ground coriander
and cumin and stir.

3 Add the drained lentils, salt and
the cup of water. Simmer gently
until the lentils start to break up
and thicken. Serve hot with a
garnish of fresh coriander
(cilantro) leaves.

BUTTER BEAN

Botanical name: *Phaseolus lunatus*
Family: *Fabaceae*

Butter beans, also known as lima beans, are members of the legume family, grown for their edible seeds which are eaten as a vegetable. The name lima bean derives from Peru's capital city of Lima, the butter bean having originated in Andean and Mesoamerican regions. It is generally believed that domestication first took place in the Andes around 2000 BC when the large-seed Lima type was first produced.

The second variety, or Sieva type, was developed in Mesoamerica in around 800 AD when a small-seeded bean was the result. By the early 1300s, cultivation had spread to North America and by the 16th century, the plant had found its way to Europe and beyond.

The term butter bean is widely used for the large, flat and yellow/white varieties (*P. lunatus var. macrocarpus*, or *P. limensis*). Butter beans have a delicate flavor that complements many dishes, and are usually bought in cans or in their dried form.

Butter beans are often added to soups and stews along with root vegetables, or they can be puréed or used to make burritos. They are often served with sweet potatoes or indeed any other meats or vegetables.

Health benefits: Butter beans, like many other legumes, are rich in dietary fiber, high in protein but low in fat, properties which enable them to regulate blood sugar levels, prevent constipation, and relieve digestive disorders and irritable bowl syndrome. Consumption of butter beans is also good for heart health, in that they lower (bad) cholesterol; they are a good source of manganese and antioxidants.

TURKISH SPICY STEW

1 tbsp olive oil
½ lb shoulder of lamb, cubed
1 onion, finely chopped
3 cloves garlic, minced
1 red chili, deseeded and minced
1 tsp cayenne pepper
3 tbsp tomato paste
4 cups lamb stock
1 medium can tomatoes, chopped
Salt and pepper to taste
2 15-oz cans butter beans
1 tsp cornstarch

Serves 2

1 Preheat the oven to 375°F. In a large skillet, heat the oil on a medium to high heat, then add the lamb and cook until lightly browned. Add the onion and garlic and cook for another few minutes.

2 Transfer to an ovenproof casserole, add the chili, cayenner, tomato paste, stock, canned tomatoes and salt and pepper. Bring to a boil, then reduce to a simmer.

3 Transfer the casserole to the oven, and cook for 1 hour.

4 Remove from the oven, add the butter beans and cornstarch, mixed to a paste in a little water, stir well, reduce the heat down a little, and cook for a further ½ hour. Check that the seasonings are correct and serve.

BLACK BEAN
Botanical name: *Phaseolus vulgaris*
Family: *Fabaceae*

Phaseolus vulgaris, or the common bean, is an herbaceous annual plant in the *Fabaceae* legume family, cultivated in many parts of the world. Numerous cultivars of green beans have been developed, but cultivars of dried (or shelling) beans from this species are even more diverse, among them the black bean or black turtle bean which, as the name implies, is dark and shiny in appearance.

Like other 'common' beans, the black bean originated in Central and South America where it was widely cultivated before it was eventually taken back to Europe by Spanish and Portuguese conquistadors.

Black beans are rich in flavor and smoky in taste. They have a velvety texture, when cooked, and make a healthy addition to the diets of vegetarians and non-vegetarians alike. Black beans are available in their canned or dried forms all year round. They can be used in a variety of ways and are a particular feature of Mexican

cuisine. In northern Mexico and in American Tex-Mex cuisine, refried beans are usually prepared with pinto beans, but many other types are used in other parts of Mexico, such as black or red beans. The raw beans can be cooked when dry or soaked overnight, then stewed, drained of most of their liquid, and converted into a paste or pressed through a fine mesh sieve. The paste is then baked or fried with lard or vegetable oil and seasoned to taste.

Health benefits: Black beans get their dark color from chemicals known as anthocyanins. These are powerful flavonoids, found in many other 'superfoods,' such as cranberries, red beets and blueberries, but which are present in larger amounts in black beans. In addition to the antioxidant properties of black beans, they are not only high in fiber, but are also credited with regulating blood sugars and lowering (bad) cholesterol. Black beans are very

low in fat, and their high fiber content makes them useful in weight-loss diets. They have good amounts of folate, which is of benefit to pregnant women, and large amounts of magnesium and iron for healthy blood cells. Black beans are a rich source of molybdenum, which some believe may help prevent cancer by protecting cells from free radicals or destructive molecules that may cause damage to cells.

MEXICAN BLACK BEAN SOUP

1 tbsp olive oil
1 onion, finely chopped
¼ lb rindless bacon, chopped
1 medium can tomatoes
2 medium red chilis, deseeded
 and chopped
2 tsp chili powder
2 tsp ground cumin
5 garlic cloves, minced
2 15-oz cans black beans, rinsed
 and drained
4 cups chicken or vegetable stock
Salt and pepper to taste

Serves 6

1 In a large pot set over a medium heat, fry the onion and bacon in the olive oil until the onion becomes translucent.

2 Add the tomatoes, chilis, chili powder, cumin and garlic and toss together over a low heat.

3 Add the beans and stock, bring to a boil, then cook at a simmer, stirring occasionally, until the soup thickens (about 1½ hours). (The soup may also be oven-cooked at 375°F for the same amount of time.) Season well and serve.

CHICKEN & BLACK BEAN BURRITOS

½ tbsp olive oil
1 cup cooked rice
2 cloves garlic, minced
½ cup water
2 tsp tomato paste
½ tsp chili powder
1 cup cooked chicken breast,
 shredded
1 15-oz can black beans
4 8-inch tortillas, warmed
½ cup grated Cheddar cheese
Salt and freshly ground black
 pepper to taste

Serves 4

1 Heat the oil in a skillet, add the rice and garlic and stir well to coat the rice. Add the water, tomato paste and chili powder, bring to a boil, then reduce to a simmer. Add the chicken and beans and continue to cook until the mixture is piping hot and the liquid evaporated.

2 Place spoonfuls of the mixture down the centers of the warmed tortillas, sprinkle with cheese, fold in the sides and roll up. Serve with a salsa or guacomole.

CRANBERRY BEAN

Botanical name: *Phaseolus vulgaris*
Family: *Fabaceae*

Cranberry beans, first cultivated in Colombia, South America, have different names that vary from country to country, e.g., the borlotti bean, also known as the Roman or romano bean (not to be confused with the Italian flat bean, a green bean bearing the same name), which is a variety of cranberry bean bred in Italy to have a thicker skin.

The beans are off-white in color, with distinctive, speckled magenta markings, and which come in beige and red pods when bought fresh. Once shelled and cooked, the cranberry bean makes a nutty, culinary treat, even though it loses its striking color and is reduced to a uniform brown. The beans are very popular in Portugal, Spain and Greece, and are of particular importance in the cuisine of Italy, where the finest beans come from the Veneto.

Fresh cranberry beans are available in the fall through to winter, but can readily be bought in their dried form from Italian grocery stores.

Cranberry beans are good in stews and soups and make a delicious addition to salads and pasta. In Italy, the beans are often served as part of an antipasto platter, accompanied by olives, cheeses and Italian salamis.

Health benefits: Cranberry beans are said to promote good kidney function. They are also high in protein which is of benefit to vegetarians and vegans. They are a good source of omega-3 and -6 fatty acids and the B-complex vitamins. They are high in fiber, which is known to lower (bad) cholesterol and helps regulate blood sugar levels. They contain important minerals such as zinc, selenium, copper, calcium, magnesium, iron and phosphorus.

CRANBERRY BEAN SALAD

4 tbsp olive oil
1 tbsp red wine vinegar
½ tsp chili powder
2 cloves garlic, minced
1 15-oz can cranberry beans,
 rinsed and drained
1 15-oz can corn kernels, drained
1 large red bell pepper, chopped
½ cup chopped flat-leaf parsley

Serves 6

1 Make a dressing in a small bowl
with the olive oil, vinegar, chili
powder and garlic.

2 Place the beans, corn, chopped
bell pepper and parsley together
in a large salad bowl, mixing the
ingredients thoroughly together.
Pour over the dressing and mix
again before serving.

NAVY BEAN

Botanical name: *Phaseolus vulgaris*
Family: *Fabaceae*

Navy beans, also known as haricot beans, Boston beans, white pea beans or pea beans, are all types of the common bean that bear the botanical name, *Phaseolus vulgaris*, most of which acquire nitrogen through a species of nitrogen-fixing bacteria.

Originally from Peru, South America, the navy bean is so-called because it was a staple food of the United States navy in the early 20th century. Nowadays, navy beans are particularly popular in America and the UK because they go to make the ubiquitous canned baked beans in tomato sauce.

Navy beans are small, oval, plump and a creamy-white in color. They are mild in flavor with a smooth, buttery texture. With little flavor of their own, they are an important ingredient in salads, soups and casseroles, making them a good vehicle for carrying other, stronger flavors. They are also cheap, help to bulk out more expensive meat, and are very nutritious and filling; they

make a excellent substitute for rice or potatoes.

Similar, and a close cousin to the navy bean, is the cannellini bean, much favored by the Italians for use in salads and the well-known Tuscan *pasta e fagioli* (pasta and beans). Another close relative is the flageolet bean, which was first developed in France in the 1800s, and which comes in a range of different cultivars. Flageolets are regarded as the 'caviar' of beans in that they are tender and full of flavor, being small, light-green and kidney-shaped, with a texture that is firm and creamy. They are particularly good served with a gigot of lamb and plenty of garlic.

Health benefits: Navy beans are full of protein, making them of particular use to vegans and vegetarians. They are also high in fiber, which is vital for healthy bowel function, protecting against constipation. Fiber also

helps to lower (bad) cholesterol levels, which improves the health of the heart in general and serves to reduce the incidence of heart attack. A high fiber diet also helps to regulate blood-sugar levels and therefore protects the body against diabetes. Navy beans are also rich in magnesium, iron, copper, manganese, folate, vitamin B1, all of which are essential to health.

HOME-MADE BAKED BEANS

3 cups navy beans
1 onion, minced
3 tbsp molasses
2 tsp salt
¼ tsp ground black pepper
¼ tsp English mustard

½ cup tomato ketchup
1 tsp Worcestershire sauce
¼ cup soft brown sugar

Serves 6

1 Prepare the beans in advance by soaking them overnight in cold water, then simmer them in the same water until tender (1–2 hours). Drain and reserve the liquid.

2 Preheat the oven to 325°F.

3 Put the drained beans into an ovenproof casserole dish. To a small pot, add the onions and sauté them for a minute or two without browning them. Stir in the molasses, salt, pepper, mustard, ketchup, Worcestershire sauce and brown sugar. Bring to a boil and pour over the beans, adding just enough of the reserved bean water to cover them.

4 Cover with a lid and bake in the oven for 3–4 hours, stirring occasionally, until the beans are tender, adding more bean water if the beans seem to be getting too dry.

SPICY BEAN & VEGETABLE STEW

1 tbsp olive oil
1 onion, chopped
3 cloves garlic, minced
1 red bell pepper, chopped
1 15-oz can chopped tomatoes
3 cups water
1 15-oz can navy beans
1 cup canned cranberry beans
1 large carrot, diced
1 sweet potato, diced
1 red chili, deseeded and finely
 chopped
1 tsp ground coriander
½–1 tsp hot chili powder
½ tsp smoked paprika (hot)
Salt to taste
2 tsp cornstarch, dissolved in 1 tsp
 cold water

Serves 4–6

1 In a large skillet or shallow pot, heat the oil and sauté the onion until translucent. Add the garlic and bell pepper and cook for another 2 minutes.

2 Add the tomatoes and water and bring to a boil. Add the rest of the ingredients (apart from the cornstarch) and bring back to a boil, then reduce to a simmer.

Cook until the carrot and sweet potato are tender.

3 Add the slaked cornstarch and stir until the stew thickens.

Continue to simmer for another 10 minutes before serving.

RED KIDNEY BEAN

Botanical name: *Phaseolus vulgaris*
Family: *Fabaceae*

Kidney beans are a member of the common bean family that includes the navy bean, cranberry bean, black bean, etc. As with many of the common beans native to Central and South America, it is generally believed that the kidney bean originated in Peru, and was then spread to other parts of Central and South America by migrating tribes. Kidney beans are striking on account of their deep red color; they are also shaped rather like kidneys as the name suggests.

Today, the beans are produced all over the world, with the largest producers being the United States, India, China, Indonesia and Brazil. Kidney beans are available all year round in both their dried and canned forms. They are very often used in dishes that are simmered, in that they readily absorb the flavors and seasonings of the other foods with which they are cooked. They also tend to hold their shape, which is useful in terms of the finished dish, and their vibrancy makes salads, soups, curries, stews and dishes with chili come to life. Kidney beans are often used as an ingredient in cakes and go well with chocolate. They are commonly used in New Orleans and much of southern Louisiana for the classic Monday Creole dish of 'red beans and rice,' while *chili con carne* is another famous dish comprising these beans. When combined with rice, kidney beans make a complete protein source of particular value to vegetarians and vegans.

Health benefits: Red kidney beans are believed to be efficaceous in cancer prevention, and beneficial for brain function, blood sugar regulation, the digestion, the cardiovascular system and bone strength. They are also low in fat and low in calories making them useful in weight-loss programs. They are high in protein and fiber and include important nutrients such as C and B-complex vitamins, and are a source of manganese, iron, phosphorus and folic acid.

CHILI CON CARNE

1 tbsp olive oil
1 large onion, chopped
4 cloves garlic, minced
2 lbs ground beef
1 large red bell pepper, chopped
1 tsp chili powder
2 tbsp unsweetened cocoa powder
2 tsp paprika
2 tbsp tomato paste
1 28-oz can chopped tomatoes
1 small bottle amber beer
1–2 cups beef stock
2 15-oz cans red kidney beans,
 drained and rinsed
1 tsp salt

Serves 6–8

1 In a large pot, heat the oil and
sweat the onion and garlic
together without browning them.
Add the ground beef and cook
until brown, then add the bell
pepper and cook for 5 minutes.

2 Add the chili powder, cocoa
powder and paprika, and stir
through the meat. Add the tomato
paste, tomatoes, beer, stock,
kidney beans and salt.

3 Bring to a boil, then simmer for
an hour, stirring occasionally. Add
more stock or water if necessary.

KIDNEY BEAN CHOCOLATE CAKE

1 15-oz can red kidney beans
1 tbsp water
1 tbsp vanilla extract
5 medium eggs
2 oz unsweetened cocoa powder
1 tsp baking powder
½ tsp baking soda
4 oz butter, softened
9 oz sugar
2 tsp espresso coffee powder

Serves 8

1 Preheat the oven to 325°F. Grease and line an 8-inch square cake pan with greaseproof paper.

2 Thoroughly rinse the kidney beans and process them in a blender into a smooth paste. Add the water, vanilla and one of the eggs and mix until smooth.

3 In a small bowl, sieve together the cocoa powder, baking powder and baking soda.

4 In a large mixing bowl, cream together the butter and sugar until pale and fluffy, then gradually beat in the remaining eggs. Add in the bean mixture and the coffee, then incorporate the cocoa mixture, mixing until smooth.

5 Pour the batter into the prepared cake pan and bake for 40–50 minutes, or until a skewer, when inserted into the cake, comes out clean.

6 Leave the cake to cool for 15 minutes before removing it from the pan. Then transfer it to a wire rack to cool completely. Top the cake with chocolate frosting and chopped nuts, or dust it with confectioner's sugar. Cut the cake into squares and serve.

PINTO BEAN
Botanical name: *Phaseolus vulgaris*
Family: *Fabaceae*

The pinto bean is the mature seed of a type of legume, closely related to other common beans, such as the navy bean, kidney bean, cranberry bean, etc., all of which are likely to have originated in Peru. They resemble kidney beans but are tan with streaks of reddish brown, which disappear once the beans are cooked. In Spanish, the bean is called the *frijol pinto*, meaning 'speckled bean' and in South America, *poroto frutilla*, literally 'strawberry bean.' The *pinto* (speckled or painted) part of the name is due to the mottled skin of the beans, which are reminiscent of the coat markings of the pinto horse.

Both canned and dried pinto beans are available throughout the year. Unlike other canned vegetables, which lose much of their goodness in the canning process, there is little difference in the nutritional value of canned pinto beans and the ones cooked at home. They can be cooked in a pressure cooker, but adding salt will make the beans tough and greatly increase the cooking time.

Pinto beans are eaten throughout the world, but not nearly as often as in Mexico and the United States, where vast quantities are consumed. For Mexican Americans, living in the United States, the pinto bean is a symbol of national identity, for it was they who introduced it to the United States. Pinto beans are also known as 'cowboy beans,' because Mexican cowboys first introduced them into Texan cuisine.

The beans may be eaten whole, mashed, or used as a filling in burritos; they are often refried and served with rice, cornbread or corn tortillas. Pinto beans make a delicious dip when blended with other ingredients, such as garlic, herbs and black pepper. In the southern United States, in poorer times, pinto beans were a winter staple, and pinto bean suppers are still enjoyed at social gatherings and fundraising events organized by churches, such are the feelings of nostalgia that are still evoked.

Health benefits: Pinto beans contain impressive amounts of vitamins and minerals, and their low fat content makes them useful additions in weight-loss programs. They are high in protein, which is essential for cell regeneration. They are very satisfying, giving a feeling of fullness in the stomach for much longer, and they are high in fiber, which helps to regulate blood sugar levels, lowers (bad) cholesterol and aids digestion. Pinto beans are a good source of iron, potassium and magnesium.

REFRIED PINTO BEANS

2 tbsp canola oil
2 15-oz cans pinto beans
2 cloves garlic, minced
1 tsp cumin powder
1 tsp chili powder
Salt to taste
Juice of ½ lime

Serves 6

1 Heat the canola oil in a skillet set over a medium heat.

2 Stir in the drained pinto beans, garlic, cumin, chili powder and a pinch of salt and cook, stirring occasionally, until the beans are thoroughly heated through (about 5 minutes).

3 Use a potato masher or fork to blend the beans to the desired texture. Check the seasoning, then add a squeeze of lime juice to the mashed beans and mix well. Use as a dip accompanied by a salsa and guacomole.

PORK & PINTO BEAN STEW

2 cups dried pinto beans (soaked and rinsed according to the pack instructions)
⅛ tsp hot pepper sauce
2 tbsp olive oil
1 large onion, chopped
2 cups cooked pork, cubed
1 tsp salt
4 garlic cloves, left whole
1¼ cups canned, chopped tomatoes
½ tsp ground marjoram
1 tsp chili powder (or to taste)

Serves 4–6

1 Using a large pot, cover the beans with water and the hot pepper sauce. Bring to a boil, reduce the heat, cover, and simmer until the beans are tender.

2 Drain the beans, but keep the cooking water.

3 In another large pot, fry the onion in the oil until golden brown. Add the beans, pork and the rest of the ingredients. Pour over the bean water, cover, and cook for about 45 minutes, stirring frequently.

SPLIT PEA

Botanical name: *Pisum sativum*
Family: *Fabaceae*

Split peas are peas that have been submitted to a mechanical process in which they are peeled, split into two and dried, the split occurring at the natural division of the seeds' cotyledons.

Dried peas have been part of the human diet since prehistoric times, and evidence of them has been found in archeological digs in Egypt, Asia and Rome. Split peas come in green and yellow varieties, the yellow having a milder flavor and the green offering an earthier, more pronounced taste. For thousands of years, dried peas were the main form in which the legume was consumed. Today, the largest commercial producers of dried

peas are Russia, France, China and Denmark.

Split peas provide a starchier, stronger-flavored legume when fresh peas are unavailable, besides being convenient to store and use. Green and yellow split peas are commonly used to make pea soup, and sometimes pease pudding, which was commonly eaten in medieval Europe. Yellow split peas are most often used to prepare dals in Guyana,

Trinidad and the Fiji Islands and are prepared in a similar way to the dals found in India. In Europe, the Greek *fava* is a dish made with yellow split peas puréed to create an appetizer or *meze*.

Health benefits: Highly nutritious, split peas are high in fiber for lowering (bad) cholesterol and regulating blood sugar levels. They also provide B-complex vitamins and phytonutrients which are a protection against heart disease.

188

THICK SPLIT PEA & HAM SOUP

1 lb yellow split peas
8 cups water
1 cup chopped onions
2 cloves garlic
1 cup chopped celery
1 tbsp olive oil
1 meaty ham bone
Salt and pepper to taste
Chopped ham to garnish

Serves 6

1 To a large pot, add the split peas and water, bring to a boil, and boil for 2 minutes. Set aside off the heat to cool for 1 hour.

2 Add the onions, garlic and celery to a food processor and blend to a smooth paste.

3 Heat the olive oil in a skillet over a gentle heat and lightly cook the paste.

4 Put the ham bone into the pot with the peas and water, then stir in the onion mixture and season well. Bring to a boil, cover, then reduce to a simmer and cook for 2½ hours, stirring occasionally.

5 Remove the ham bone from the soup and discard. Check the seasoning and serve in separate bowls garnished with the pieces of chopped ham.

FAVA BEAN/BROAD BEAN

Botanical name: *Vicia faba*
Family: *Fabaceae*

Vicia faba is also known as the broad bean, faba bean, field bean, bell bean or tic bean. Native to North Africa and south-west Asia, it is now extensively cultivated throughout the world. The cultivation of the fava bean dates back to ancient time, where it was grown throughout the fertile valleys of the eastern Mediterranean and was also a staple food source of the ancient Greeks and Romans.

Fava beans are tolerant of harsh conditions, making them very easy to grow and they also act as a cover crop which serves to reduce soil erosion. Like all beans, they are nitrogen fixers, which allows them to rejuvenate the soil with this particular nutrient.

The beans are usually sown in spring to mature throughout the summer, being at their peak in midsummer. They possess attractive pinkish-white flowers which are attractive to honey bees. Unlike green beans, where the

and creamy texture, this versatile bean can be used in numerous ways, such as in soups, stews, salads and stir-fries; they go particularly well with lamb, poultry and seafood.

Health benefits: Fava beans are a nutrient-rich legume high in protein and fiber but very low in fat. They are bursting with health-giving antioxidants, vitamins and minerals. Dietary fiber has been shown to reduce (bad) cholesterol and can help protect the body from some cancers, particularly colon cancer. Fava beans are an excellent source of B-complex vitamins, including folates, and are loaded with nutrients such as iron, copper, manganese, calcium and magnesium.

whole seed pod can be eaten, fava beans have an extremely thick, inedible and indigestible cover which is removed to extract the broad, thick, flat seeds (beans) inside. Fava beans are full of flavor and are meaty enough to be served on their own or as a side dish. They are well-known in Mediterranean cuisine and are usually served in season during the summer months. Fortunately, they can still be eaten all-year-round in canned, frozen or dried forms. With their distinctive flavor

FAVA BEAN & POACHED EGG SALAD

1 cup fresh podded or frozen fava beans
1 cup trimmed green beans
2 tbsp olive oil
2 tbsp white wine vinegar
Salt and pepper to taste
A handful of mixed salad leaves
8 grape tomatoes, halved
2 eggs
Freshly ground black pepper

Serves 2

1 Cook both the fava and the green beans togther in a large pot of boiling water until *al dente*. Remove from the heat, drain, and allow to cool.

2 Make a dressing with the oil, vinegar, salt and pepper.

3 Take two plates and build up the salad, starting with the leaves, then the tomatoes, green beans and fava beans. Drizzle the dressing over the top.

4 Cook two soft poached eggs, placing them on top of the salad. Finish with a grind of black pepper over the eggs.

PASTA WITH FAVA BEAN SAUCE

2 cups fresh podded or frozen fava
 beans
8 oz macaroni or similar pasta
½ cup freshly grated Parmesan
 cheese
2 tbsp unsalted butter
2 garlic cloves, minced
¼ cup half-and-half
1 tbsp fresh lemon juice
2 tbsp olive oil
Salt and black pepper to taste

Serves 4

1 Cook the fava beans in boiling
salted water until tender, then
drain and set them aside.

2 Cook the pasta in boiling salted
water until *al dente*.

3 While the pasta is cooking, put
the rest of the ingredients,
including the fava beans, into a
food processor and blend until
smooth.

4 Strain the pasta and return it to
the pot. Add the bean sauce and
stir over a low heat to make both
pasta and sauce piping hot.

ADZUKI BEAN
Botanical name: *Vigna angularis*
Family: *Fabaceae*

Adzuki can also be spelt azuki or aduki, depending on how the word is translated from the Japanese. The adzuki bean is an annual vine grown throughout East Asia and the Himalayas. Although originally from China, where the beans are widely consumed, they are very popular in Japan and in both countries are eaten on ceremonial occasions. Usually, the beans are a uniform red color with a sweet, nutty taste, although there are other varieties which can be white, gray, black or mottled.

In Asian cuisine, the adzuki bean is usually eaten in a sweetened form, often boiled in sugar which results in a red bean paste; this is then used in a wide range of dishes and often served

with rice. A more liquid version, using adzuki beans boiled with water, sugar and a little salt, produces a sweet dish known as red bean soup. In addition, adzuki beans are commonly made into a tea-like drink and the beans can also be sprouted.

Adzuki beans are also used as a topping for sweet buns, biscuits or pastries. To appeal to Western tastes, adzuki beans can be made into veggie burgers or added to salads along with other wholesome ingredients.

Heath benefits: Adzuki beans are an excellent source of dietary fiber which helps to lower (bad) cholesterol. They contain good amounts of folate, potassium and magnesium, which are essential for cardiovascular health. The high fiber element also helps protect the digestive system by preventing constipation and colon cancer, while the fiber maintains a satisfied feeling for longer, making it helpful in weight-loss programs. Adzuki beans are a good source of B-complex vitamins as well as other trace elements such as copper, zinc and manganese.

ZENZAI (Rice Dumplings in a Sweet Bean Soup)

1 cup adzuki beans
1¼ cups sugar
6 cups water
½ tsp salt
16 oz sweet rice mochi flour

Serves 4

1 Prepare the adzuki beans by soaking them overnight in water. Discard the soaking water, then place the beans and the 6 cups of water in a pot and bring to a boil. Reduce the heat and simmer for 2 hours until the beans are soft. (During cooking, a good deal of water will be absorbed, so add more to the pan so that the bean mixture produces about 5 cups.) Add the sugar and salt and cook for a further 20 minutes, stirring occasionally.

2 Meanwhile, prepare the dumplings. Place the mochi in a bowl and add water, a little at a time, until a stiff dough forms. Roll out until the dough is about ½ inch thick, then cut into 8 squares.

3 Bring the adzuki beans back to a boil, then drop the mochi squares into the soup. Cook until the mochi rise to the surface. Divide the soup and mochi into four bowls and serve hot.

ADZUKI JELLO

1 cup adzuki beans
¼ tsp bicarbonate of soda
2¾ pints water
½ cup sugar
2 tbsp vanilla extract
1 tbsp superfine sugar
2 packages powdered gelatine
Pinch of salt

Serves 4–6

1 Soak the beans overnight in cold water so that they are completely submerged. Drain and rinse thoroughly.

2 In a heavy-bottomed pot, bring the 2¾ pints water to a boil over a high heat. Turn the heat to low, then add the bicarbonate of soda, the beans and a pinch of salt. Stir, then partially cover to allow the steam to escape. Simmer for 2 hours until the beans are soft.

3 Remove from the heat and pour the contents of the pot into a food processor, blending everything to a smooth purée. Return the purée to the pot and stir in the sugar and vanilla extract.

4 On a low heat, simmer the purée, stirring, until it is reduced to a paste. (On no account must the paste be allowed to stick.)

5 Remove the red bean paste from the heat. Next, pour ½ cup of water into a small pot, add the superfine sugar and the gelatine, and simmer gently for a few minutes, stirring constantly, until the sugar and gelatine have completely dissolved. Stir into the hot bean paste, mixing very thoroughly.

6 Rinse the inside of a small, rectangular dish with cold water and fill it with the mixture. Gently tap the bottom of the dish on the worktop to make the contents settle and smooth the surface with a palette knife. Leave to set at room temperature, then refrigerate until required.

7 To serve the jelly, run the blade of a knife around the inside of the dish, then turn the jelly out onto a board and cut it into squares. Serve with vanilla ice cream.

MUNG BEAN

Botanical name: *Vigna radiata*
Family: *Fabaceae*

The mung bean is also known as
the moong bean, green soy bean
and green gram. It is a small green
legume native to the Indian
subcontinent, although it is widely
cultivated today in India, China,
South-East Asia and the hotter
parts of southern Europe and the
United States.

Mung beans are small and oval
in shape and known for their
sweet flavor. They are usually
green but can be yellow or black.
Mung beans are extensively used
in Asian cuisine, and they can be
eaten as beans, left to sprout, and
even ground into flour. The
ancient Chinese utilized mung

beans for medicinal purposes as well as in their cusine, using them for dispelling heat and detoxifying the body.

In cooking, mung beans have savory as well as sweet applications. Unlike many other beans, they are easy to digest and do not cause undue flatulence. They are a popular alternative to meat for vegetarians, in that a complete protein is formed when combined with cereals.

Health benefits: Mung beans are low in cholesterol but high in dietary fiber, making them of benefit to those with raised cholesterol levels. They are good for the digestive and cardiovascular systems and for post-menopausal women. Mung beans are also thought to protect the body from some cancers and promote healthy blood-sugar levels. They are high in proteins, rich in B-complex, C and K vitamins, and contain many essential nutrients required for the proper functioning of the body.

SPROUTED MUNG BEAN SALAD

1 lb well-rinsed mung bean
 sprouts
½ tsp salt
2 tbsp white vinegar
2 tbsp sesame oil
1 tbsp sugar
Salt and pepper to taste

Serves 4–6

1 Bring about 2 quarts water to a
boil in a large pot. Add the bean
sprouts and salt, and cook until
the sprouts begin to wilt slightly
while retaining a slight crunch
(4 to 5 minutes). Drain the sprouts
well, pour into a bowl, and leave
to cool. Refrigerate for ½ hour.

2 Make a dressing from the
vinegar, sesame oil, sugar, and salt
and pepper to taste. Refrigerate
for ½ hour.

3 Put the sprouts into a serving
bowl, then pour over the dressing
and gently mix through.

MUNG BEANS & VEGETABLES

1 cup uncooked mung beans
4 large potatoes, peeled and diced
1 tbsp olive oil
1 onion, finely chopped
2 cloves garlic, minced
2 carrots, diced
2 cups chicken or vegetable stock
Salt and black pepper to taste
4 tomatoes, quartered
3 tbsp chopped parsley

Serves 6–8

1 Preheat the oven to 400°F.

2 In a small pot, cover the mung beans with water and bring them to a boil, then reduce the heat and simmer them for 20 minutes. Drain the beans, rinse them under cold water, then set aside.

3 In another pot, parboil the potatoes in salted water. Drain, then cover and set aside.

4 Heat the oil in a skillet set over a medium heat. Add the onion and sauté until translucent. Add the garlic and carrots and cook for

about 5 minutes. Pour the vegetables, potatoes, beans and stock into an ovenproof casserole, season to taste and stir through.

5 Cover with a lid and bake in the oven for 20 minutes or so until the mixture is bubbling hot. Remove from the oven and stir in the tomatoes, then return to the oven and cook for another 10 minutes.

Garnish with the chopped parsley and serve.

BLACK-EYED PEA

Botanical name: *Vigna unguiculata*
Family: *Fabaceae*

The black-eyed pea, also known as the black-eyed bean in some English-speaking countries, is a legume and a subspecies of the cowpea. The most commercially grown variety is the California blackeye, which is a pale creamy-white in color with a black spot along one side. A common variation of the black-eyed pea is the purple hull pea, which is usually green with a purple or pink spot. It is believed that the black-eyed pea originated in North Africa or Asia where it has been part of the indigenous diet for around 5,000 years.

The legume was introduced into the Indian diet as much as 3,000 years ago and was also a staple of the ancient Greeks and Romans. It is understood that it found its way from Africa to the Americas by way of Spanish explorers and the slave trade, becoming a staple food throughout the American South and also in the West Indies.

Black-eyed peas are a symbol of good luck, wealth and prosperity in the United States, and are traditionally eaten on New Year's Day, especially in the southern states, where at least 365 of them must be eaten on this day to ensure good luck throughout the coming year. Hoppin' John is the traditional African-American recipe eaten on this day and is as important today as it has always been. There are other good luck traditions connected with black-eyed peas, such as those celebrated at the Jewish New Year. Black-eyed peas are often served with cornbread and vegetables such as collard greens, mustard or turnip greens and cabbage.

Heath benefits: There are a great many health benefits associated with black-eyed peas: they are very high in fiber, which is essential for maintaining a healthy digestive system; they help to regulate blood sugar levels, benefiting diabetics; they lower (bad) cholesterol and are a good source of folate which plays a vital role in building cells and is so important in the formation of healthy embryos.

Black-eyed peas are high in protein, which is essential for healthy muscles and bones. They are a good source of the B-complex and E vitamins, and are rich in iron, phosphorus, manganese and potassium. They are good for weight-loss in that they are satisfying but relatively low in calories. They benefit the heart and bladder and have anti-cancer properties.

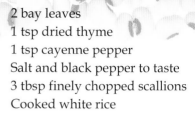

HOPPIN' JOHN

1 tbsp olive oil
1 large ham hock
1 cup chopped onion
½ cup chopped celery

½ cup chopped green pepper
1 tbsp chopped garlic
1 lb black-eyed peas, soaked
  overnight and rinsed
1 qt chicken stock

2 bay leaves
1 tsp dried thyme
1 tsp cayenne pepper
Salt and black pepper to taste
3 tbsp finely chopped scallions
Cooked white rice

Serves 6–8

1 Heat the oil in a large pot, add the ham hock and brown it all over. Add the onion, celery, green pepper and garlic and cook for a few minutes until soft but not browned. Add the black-eyed peas, the stock, the bay leaves, thyme, cayenne and salt and pepper.

2 Bring to a boil, reduce the heat, then simmer for 40 minutes or so until the peas are tender, adding more water or stock if necessary.

3 Remove the ham hock and cut the meat into bite-sized pieces, returning them to the pot with the peas. Check the seasonings and serve the peas over the cooked rice, adding a sprinkling of the chopped scallions over the top.

SPICY THREE BEAN SOUP

2 tbsp olive oil

½ onion, diced

1 clove garlic, minced

2 sticks celery, diced

1 fresh red chili, deseeded and
 minced

2 tsp chili powder

2 tbsp tomato purée

2 cups canned black-eyed peas,
 rinsed and drained

2 cups canned red kidney beans,
 rinsed and drained

2 cups canned navy beans,
 rinsed and drained

1 tbsp brown sugar

2 cups water

1 vegetable bouillon cube

1 bay leaf

2 tbsp cornstarch

½ cup red wine

Serves 6–8

1 Heat the olive oil in a large pot over a medium heat. Sauté the onion until translucent, then add the garlic and cook for another minute or so.

2 Add the celery, chili, chili powder, tomato purée, the peas and beans, the sugar, water, vegetable bouillon cube, bay leaf, and bring to a boil.

3 Dissolve the cornstarch in a little water. Turn down the heat to a simmer and mix the cornstarch into the soup to thicken it slightly. Stir in the red wine and continue to simmer for approx 30 minutes before serving.

NUTS

CASHEW NUT

Botanical name: *Anacardium occidentale*
Family: *Anacardiaceae*

The cashew is a tropical evergreen tree indigenous to the north-eastern Brazilian rainforest, where its fruit, the cashew apple, is a highly-prized delicacy. What we call the cashew nut is actually the seed from this fruit and, unlike most fruits where the seed is found inside the flesh, the cashew nut hangs from the bottom of the cashew apple. The kidney-shaped cashew is a close relative of the pistachio, mango, poison ivy and poison oak.

In the main, the cashew seed is treated as a nut. It is delicately sweet, yet crunchy with a unique texture. Its use in cooking was spread worldwide during the 16th century, when Portuguese exporers introduced it to other cultures. Cashews can be roasted, sugared, used in appetizers, main meals, stir-fry dishes, salads and desserts.

208

Cashews are always sold with their shells removed because the shells contain a caustic resin that is poisonous and can burn the skin. These are not wasted, however, as the shells have industrial applications in the manufacture of paints, varnishes and insecticides.

Because the cashew is not a true nut, it has been found that people who are intolerant or allergic to nuts can still eat cashews.

Health benefits: Studies have shown that cashews can not only reduce the risk of colon cancer but also protect the body against other cancers and cardiovascular disorders. Cashews contain monounsaturated fats, which are also found in olive oil, and which help to protect the heart and help regulate cholesterol levels. Cashews are rich in many minerals and other nutrients which promote healthy hair and skin and also encourages strong bones. They are good for the nervous system and offer protection against gallstones. Being high in fiber, they are also of value in weight management.

THAI CHICKEN WITH CASHEW NUTS

2 tbsp vegetable oil
4 oz unroasted cashew nuts
2 hot chili peppers, seeded
 and finely sliced
4 dried red chilis, left whole
1¼ lbs boneless, skinless chicken
 breasts, cut into slices
5 tbsp light soy sauce
5 tbsp Thai fish sauce
1 tbsp white sugar
1 cup sliced snow peas
1 red bell pepper, sliced
½ red onion, sliced
Thai basil to garnish

Serves 4

1 Heat the oil in a wok and add
the cashews. Once browned,
transfer the cashews to a bowl and
set aside.

2 Add the fresh and
dried chilis to the wok
and cook for 20 seconds.
Stir in the chicken and cook
for about 5 minutes.

3 Stir in the soy sauce, fish sauce,
and sugar. Stir-fry for another 5
minutes or so until the chicken is
cooked through. Stir in the snow
peas, bell peppers, red onion and
and cook for a few minutes, then
add the cashews and heat
thoroughly. Serve with a garnish
of Thai basil leaves.

ARUGULA, PEAR & CASHEW SALAD

FOR THE SALAD:

1 pear, cored and sliced
1 cup pre-washed arugula leaves
½ cup cashew nuts

FOR THE DRESSING:

1 tbsp extra virgin olive oil
1 tbsp balsamic vinegar
Salt and pepper to taste

Serves 2

Carefully arrange the salad ingredients on a serving plate, drizzle with the prepared dressing, then serve.

PEANUT

Botanical name: *Arachis hypogaea*
Family: *Fabaceae*

The peanut, also known as the ground nut, is a species in the legume or bean family, making it technically not a nut at all. It is thought that peanuts were first cultivated in the valleys of Paraguay and Bolivia, where the wildest strains currently grow. Peanuts played an important role in the diets of cultures such as the Aztecs and other civilizations native to Central and South America, and the Moche, another

pre-Columbian people, actually depicted peanuts in their art. Peanuts were eventually spread worldwide by European traders.

Peanuts grow in an interesting way: they start off as an above-ground flower that, due to its heavy weight, bends toward the ground. The flower eventually burrows underground, which is where the peanut matures.

There are a number of varieties of peanut, the most common being the Virginia, Spanish and Valencia. Due to their high protein content and chemical profile, they are processed into a variety of different forms, including butter, oil, flour and flakes. In the kitchen, peanuts can be added to salads, chicken or vegetable dishes, to many Asian dishes, or end up as peanut butter.

Even though peanuts are almost ubiquitous throughout the world, they have come to be associated with severe allergic reactions in some people and particularly in children. A peanut allergy can produce a wide range of symptoms, from a minor irritation to life-threatening anaphylactic shock. It is therefore of utmost importance to obtain medical advice, even if the reaction is minor, and to avoid anything to which peanuts may have been added.

Health benefits: Peanuts are a good energy food and a source of many of the nutrients, minerals and antioxidants essential for good health. They have sufficient levels of monounsaturated fats, especially oleic acid, which are known to lower (bad) cholesterol and help prevent arterial disease and stroke. Peanuts are reputed to prevent some cancers, degenerative nerve disease, gallstones, Alzehimer's disease and viral or fungal infections. The kernels are an excellent source of B-complex and E vitamins and minerals, such as copper, manganese, potassium, calcium, iron, magnesium, zinc and selenium.

SATAY CHICKEN

2 tbsp smooth peanut butter
½ cup soy sauce
½ cup lime juice
1 tbsp brown sugar
2 tbsp curry powder
2 cloves garlic, chopped
1 tsp hot pepper sauce
6 skinless, boneless chicken
 breasts cubed
Lime wedges

Serves 2

1 In a mixing bowl, combine the
peanut butter, soy sauce, lime
juice, brown sugar, curry powder,
garlic and hot pepper sauce.
Cover the chicken cubes in this
marinade and refrigerate for at
least 2 hours or preferably
overnight.

2 Preheat a broiler to a high heat,
or a barbecue may be used.

3 Thread chicken cubes onto
skewers that have been presoaked
in water, and grill or barbecue
them for 5 minutes on each side
or until the chicken is thoroughly
cooked through. Serve wedges
of lime.

PEANUT BRITTLE

1 cup white sugar
½ cup light corn syrup
¼ tsp salt
¼ cup water
1 cup peanuts
1 tbsp softened butter
1 tsp baking soda

1 Grease and line a large cookie sheet with a silicone baking mat or buttered baking parchment.

2 In a heavy pot set over a medium heat, bring to a boil the sugar, corn syrup, salt and water. Shake the pot until the sugar is dissolved, then add the peanuts.

Place a candy thermometer in the mixture and keep it there until it registers 300°F.

3 Remove from the heat and stir in the butter and baking soda. Pour out onto the prepared cookie sheet and let it spread out. Cool, then snap the brittle into pieces.

BRAZIL NUT

Botanical name: *Bertholletia excelsa*
Family: *Lecythidaceae*

The Brazil nut tree is native to the non-flooded forests of the Guianas, Venezuela, Brazil, Colombia, Peru and Bolivia, where it occurs along river banks of the Amazon, Rio Negro, Tapajós and Orinoco. It is related to other well-known plants, such as blueberries, cranberries, sapote, tea, gooseberries, phlox and persimmons.

The Brazil nut is a large tree that can attain 160 ft, making it one of the largest trees in the Amazon rainforest, and it can live for 500 years or more. The stem is straight and commonly without branches

for well over half of the tree's height, with an emergent crown of branches above and a surrounding canopy. The fruit of the tree resembles a 4–6-lb coconut and can hold as many as 30 Brazil nuts within.

Native Amazonians have cherished the delicious Brazil nut throughout the ages, for it has provided a much-needed supply of protein, fats and other essential nutrients. Today, rather surprisingly, Bolivia is the largest producer of Brazil nuts and is responsible for a good half of the world's production.

In Brazil, in an effort to support their conservation, the trees are protected and it is illegal to cut them down. The Brazil nut tree also struggles to grow, away from its natural habitat, in that it requires a specific species of bee to pollinate it that can only survive in a particular natural environment.

Brazil nuts may be eaten as they are or they can be enjoyed roasted, salted or sweetened. They are often used in fudges, puddings, pestos and chocolate bars, and are an important ingredient in fruitcakes; they can be added to salads, meat dishes and soups, while Brazil nut oil is often used in salad dressings and in cooking. Like other nuts, Brazils are known to cause allergies in some individuals which can range from simple reactions, such as skin itching, to more serious anaphylactic manifestations.

Health benefits: Brazil nuts are highly calorific but, like many other nuts, the fat content is monounsaturated, which is known to lower (bad) cholesterol and increase the good. Brazil nuts are of benefit to the cardiovascular system and can help prevent stroke. They have exceptionally high levels of selenium, which protects the body agains coronary artery disease, liver cirrhosis and some cancers. Brazils are high in vitamin E and contain other important B-complex vitamins. They have good levels of copper, magnesium, manganese, potassium, calcium, iron, phosphorus and zinc.

217

DARK CHOCOLATE BRAZIL NUT MOUSSE

4¼ oz dark chocolate, broken into
 pieces
3½ oz shelled Brazil nuts
¾ cup heavy cream
2 egg whites
2 tbsp sugar
Chocolate shavings

Serves 4–6

1 Grind the nuts to a fine powder
in a food processor.

2 Put the chocolate into a bowl
and place the bowl over a pot of
water, with the water not touching
the bowl. (Use a double boiler if
you have one.) Bring the pot of
water to a boil, then simmer until
the chocolate in the bowl is
melted. Turn off the heat, leaving
the chocolate to keep warm.

3 Divide the cream into half in two
separate bowls. Heat one of the
halves over a low flame until
bubbles start to appear, but on no
account let it boilAway from its
natural habitat, .

4 Add this cream to the bowl of
chocolate and leave to stand.

5 Whip the egg whites and sugar
together until stiff. Add the egg-
white foam to the warm chocolate
and cream mixture and gently
mix, using a folding method, until
no white streaks remain.

6 Stir the Brazil nut flour into the
chocolate and mix well.

7 Whip the remaining cream (the
second bowl) into soft peaks that
hold their shape. Pour the cream
into the chocolate mixture and
fold in gently.

8 Pour the mousse into serving
glasses or cups and leave to set in
the refrigerator for a few hours.
Garnish with chocolate shavings
before serving.

CHESTNUT

Botanical name: *Castanea sativa*
Family: *Fagaceae*

The sweet chestnut tree, sometimes called the chestnut, is a species of flowering plant native to Europe and Asia, but which is widely cultivated throughout the world where temperate climates prevail. Botanically, the nuts belong to the beech or *Fagaceae* family, in the genus *Castanea*.

The sweet chestnut is a long-lived deciduous tree that produces an edible seed known as the chestnut. The raw nuts, though edible, have a skin which is astringent and unpleasant to eat when still moist; after drying for a time the thin skin loses its astringency but is better removed to reach the white fruit beneath.

Chestnuts are traditionally roasted in their tough brown

husks after removing the spiny cupules in which they grow on the tree, the husks having been peeled off and discarded and the hot chestnuts dipped in salt before eating them. Roast chestnuts are traditionally sold in markets and fairgrounds by street vendors with mobile or static braziers.

Once cooked, chestnuts are sweet in flavor and floury in texture. They can be used in puddings, desserts, cakes or as a stuffing for poultry.

Health benefits: Chestnuts are relatively low in calories but rich in many other nutrients essential to good health and have an abundance of mono-unsaturated fats. They are a good source of dietary fiber, which helps regulate cholesterol. They are exceptionally rich in B-complex and C vitamins, which are strong antioxidants offering protection against free radicals. Chestnuts are rich in folates which is unusual for nuts. They are a good souce of iron, calcium, magnesium, manganese, phosphorus, potassium and zinc. As chestnuts are gluten-free they are a good alternative food source for celiac disease sufferers or for those who are gluten-sensitive.

SWEET CHESTNUT SOUP

4 tbsp unsalted butter
1 parsnip, finely chopped
1 stick celery, finely chopped
½ medium onion, finely chopped
2 cups cooked chestnuts
 (can be obtained vacuum-packed)
1 cup dry sherry
3 cups chicken or vegetable
 stock
½ cup heavy cream
Salt and pepper to taste

Serves 4

1 Melt the butter in a medium-sized pot. Add the parsnip, celery and onion and sauté over a low-medium heat for about 10 minutes until the vegetables are soft but not browned.

2 Add the chestnuts and continue to cook for 4 minutes. Add the sherry and cook over a medium heat until the sherry is reduced by half (about 4 minutes). Add the stock and bring to a boil.

3 Partially cover the pot and simmer over a low heat for 30 minutes.

4 Add the cream, then purée the soup in a blender in batches. Return the soup to the pot to reheat it gently. Season with salt and pepper and top with a few toasted croutons.

ROASTED SWEET CHESTNUTS

1 lb fresh unshelled chestnuts

1 Bring a medium-sized pot of water to a boil, then turn off the heat.

2 Leave the chestnuts in the hot water to soak for 1 minute, then drain and pat them dry. (This softens the chestnuts, making them easier to score.)

3 Using a sharp paring knife, carefully cut slits on the rounded sides of each chestnut, but do not cut into the meat beneath.

4 Arrange the nuts, slit sides up, in a single layer in a heavy skillet on the stovetop, or, more traditionally, place them on a shovel in the embers of a real fire. Roast the chestnuts over a medium heat until the shells split open at the cuts (about 15–20 minutes).

5 Peel the chestnuts when they are comfortable to handle (they will be harder to peel if left to cool completely).

PECAN

Botanical name: *Carya illinoinensis*
Family: *Juglandaceae*

The pecan tree is a species of hickory (*Juglandaceae*) native to Mexico and the south-central and south-eastern United States. For thousands of years, pecans were an important staple in the indigenous food supply, and it was the Native Americans themselves who taught early European colonists how to harvest, store and utilize these nutrient-rich nuts. Today, the pecan is cultivated in other regions of the world as an important commercial crop, with Israel, Australia and South Africa all having sizeable operations.

The tree itself is large and deciduous and bears 'nuts' which are technically drupes rather that nuts, and which are fruits with a single stone or pit surrounded by a husk. The word 'pecan' comes from the Algonquian indicating that it requires a stone to crack it.

The versatile pecan nut has a rich, buttery flavor. It can be eaten as it comes or used in cooking, particularly in sweet desserts and pastries. One of the most famous desserts is pecan pie, which is a traditional dish of America's southern states. Pecans are also a main ingredient in the making of praline, and wood from the pecan tree is traditionally used in furniture-making and flooring and as a fuel for flavoring and smoking meats.

Health benefits: Pecan nuts offer unique health benefits. They are renowned for their vitamin E antioxidant qualities, which scientists claim protect the body from neurological and coronary heart disease, while their other phytochemical properties protect against cancer and infections. Pecans are extremely rich in

manganese, which is known to protect the heart, and also contain other nutrients such as zinc, phosphorus, iron, calcium and selenium. Pecans are packed with fatty acids, among them oleic acid, which is an aid to weight control and helps to lower (bad) cholesterol.

PECAN PIE WITH MAPLE SYRUP

PASTRY CASE:
1 cup all-purpose flour
Pinch of salt
2 tbsp sugar
¼ cup vegetable shortening
1½ tbsp cold butter, cut into small
 pieces
3 tbsp ice water

FILLING:
4 large eggs
⅔ cup sugar
½ cup pure maple syrup
½ cup light corn syrup
6 tbsp unsalted butter, melted
1 cup coarsely chopped pecans
Pecan halves to decorate

Serves 6–8

1 Preheat the oven to 450°F.

2 Place the flour, salt and sugar in a food processor and pulse to combine. Add the shortening and butter and pulse until the mixture resembles coarse breadcrumbs, with a few pea-sized pieces of butter still visible. Sprinkle with 1 tablespoonful of the ice water, and pulse until the dough becomes crumbly but holds together when squeezed. (Add more of the water, a little at a time, only if necessary, and do not overprocess.) Form the dough into a disk, wrap it in plastic and refrigerate for 1 hour.

3 On a lightly floured surface, roll out the dough to fit a greased 10-inch pie pan. Prick the bottom of the pie shell with a fork, then line the bottom with greaseproof paper. Add some dried beans, then bake blind until lightly colored (about 10 minutes). Next, bake for a further 10 minutes with the paper and beans removed, until the pie crust is a light golden brown. Cool, then gently trim off the excess crust to make a smooth edge. Reduce the oven to 350°F.

4 In a medium bowl, whisk together the eggs and sugar until well-blended. Stir in the maple and corn syrups, then the butter and pecans. Pour the filling into the pre-baked pie shell and bake for 30–35 minutes. (If the crust becomes too brown after 30 minutes, cover the pie lightly with foil.) Decorate the top of the pie with the pecan halves and leave to cool on a wire rack before serving.

COCONUT

Botanical name: *Cocos nucifera*
Family: *Arecaceae*

The coconut palm is a member of the *Arecaceae* family and is the only accepted species in the genus *Cocos*. The word comes from the 16th-century Portuguese and Spanish *coco*, meaning 'head' or 'skull.' The coconut is found in both tropical and subtropical regions of the world.

The coconut has been justly valued for thousands of years for its great versatility, as apparent in the many domestic, commercial and industrial applications of its different constituents. Coconuts are different from other fruits in that they contain large

quantities of 'water' and, when immature, are known as tender-nuts or jelly-nuts and may be harvested for drinking. When mature, they still contain some water and can be used as seednuts or processed to produce oil from the kernels, charcoal from the hard shells and coir from the fibrous husks.

The coconut is an important part of the daily diet of many people throughout the world. The Pacific islanders believe the coconut to be a cure-all, which is

228

why it is known to them as 'the tree of life.'

Coconut oil is rich in saturated fat in the form of medium-chain triglycerides, which gives it the impressive shelf-life but raises fears regarding its health implications. It is claimed, however, that vegetable oils, such as sunflower, soya and corn, are not ideal for cooking, in that they tend to suffer heat damage and therefore oxidization; coconut oil, on the other hand, is very stable, and because it does not need to go through partial hydrogenation, contains no transfats. Consult your doctor before using coconut oil you have any misgivings.

Health benefits: Although high in saturated fat, coconut is thought to benefit diabetes, Crohn's disease, irritable bowel syndrome (IBS), Alzheimer's disease, thyroid conditions and the immune system. It contains A and B-complex vitamins, folate, iron, zinc, phosphorus, magnesium, potassium, calcium and antioxidants.

COCONUT CUPCAKES

CUPCAKES:
¾ cup room-temperature unsalted butter
1¼ cups sugar
3 room-temperature eggs
1¼ cups flour
Pinch of salt
1 tsp baking powder
1 cup canned coconut milk
1 tsp vanilla extract
½ cup sweetened desiccated coconut

Makes 20 cupcakes

COCONUT FROSTING:
½ cup room-temperature butter
1 cup room-temperature cream cheese
1 cup sugar
¼ cup sweetened desiccated coconut

MAKE THE CUPCAKES:
1 Preheat the oven to 350°F. In a mixing bowl, cream together the butter and sugar until light and pale in color, scraping down the sides of the bowl halfway through to ensure even mixing.

2 Add the eggs, one at a time, beating them well in.

3 Combine the flour, salt and baking powder in another bowl, then add 1 cupful of a well-shaken can of coconut milk and a teaspoonful of vanilla to a third bowl. Add a third of the dry ingredients and mix, then add half the wet ingredients. Continue adding alternating wet and dry mixtures, ending up with the dry. Stop mixing as soon as the ingredients are fully incorporated. Fold in the desiccated coconut.

4 Line a muffin pan with paper liners, then fill each liner to the top with the batter. Bake for 25–35 minutes until the tops are brown and a skewer, when inserted into a cake, comes out clean. Allow to cool in the pan for 15 minutes, then remove to a baking rack and leave to cool completely.

MAKE THE COCONUT FROSTING:
1 Cream the butter and cream cheese together, scraping down

the sides of the bowl as you go. Slowly add the sugar, tasting as you go until the desired sweetness is obtained.

2 Fold in the desiccated coconut, then spread the frosting onto the cooled cupcakes, sprinkling on a little extra coconut to finish.

COCONUT & BANANA SMOOTHIE

1 cup coconut milk
½ cup apple juice
½ cup ice
½ cup coconut flesh, chopped into small pieces
½ banana

Serves 2

In a food processor, blend the coconut milk and ice with the banana until slushy. Add the apple juice and coconut flesh and blend until thoroughly mixed in, remembering that it is the texture of the coconut that adds to the enjoyment of the smoothie.

HAZELNUT

Botanical name: *Corylus avellana*
Family: *Betulaceae or Corylaceae*

Corylus avellana, the common hazel, is a species of shrub native to Europe and Asia. It is cultivated for its nuts, which are also known as cob nuts or filberts. References to the hazel have been found in Chinese manuscripts dating back 5,000 years and it is known that the ancient Greeks and Romans used the nuts for medicinal purposes.

The kernel of the seed is edible and is eaten raw or roasted, or it can be ground into a paste. The hazelnut is shaped like an acorn and has an outer husk that opens as the nut matures. The hazel tree produces fruits about three years after planting, and in spring bears

attractive catkins consisting of flowers arranged along a central stem which ultimately develop into fruits by the fall.

Today, the main producers of hazelnuts are Turkey, Italy, Spain and France, while in the United States they are mainly grown in Oregan and Washington, where they are an important commercial crop.

Hazelnuts are good to eat on their own or they can be roasted, salted or sweetened. They are widely used in confectionary, particularly that which contains chocolate, and are also an ingredient in cakes and other dessert recipes.

Health benefits: Hazelnuts are a high-energy food loaded with health-giving nutrients that are essential for good health. They are rich in monounsaturated fats, such as oleic and linoleic acid, which are good for cardiovascular health and for lowering (bad) cholesterol. They are also high in dietary fiber and packed with vitamins and minerals, which together help to prevent many diseases, including cancers. Hazelnuts are particularly rich in vitamin E, which is a powerful antioxidant, also folates and the other B-complex vitamins. They are loaded with manganese, potassium, calcium, copper, iron, magnesium, zinc and selenium.

HAZELNUT & DATE LOAF CAKE

1 cup softened butter
1 cup granulated sugar
2 tbsp vanilla sugar
4 medium eggs
1¾ cups self-raising flour
1 tsp baking powder
1 cup roughly-chopped hazelnuts
2 cups pitted and chopped dates
1 tbsp brandy
2 tbsp mixed seeds and nuts for
 the topping

1 Preheat the oven to 350°F, then grease and line a 9 x 5-inch loaf pan.

2 In a large bowl, beat the butter, sugar and vanilla sugar together until pale and fluffy.

3 Beat in the eggs, one at a time.

4 Sift together the flour and baking powder, then fold into the butter mixture, combining thoroughly.

5 Gently stir in the hazelnuts, dates and brandy.

6 Turn the batter into the greased loaf pan, sprinkling the top with the mixed seeds and nuts.

7 Bake for 60–70 minutes or until a skewer, inserted in the middle of the loaf, comes out clean. Remove from the pan and leave to cool on a wire rack.

TIP: Delicious served with cream cheese and fresh fruit.

235

HAZELNUT PANFORTE

1¼ cups chopped figs or dates (pits removed)

2 tbsp honey

½ cup soft brown sugar

½ tsp each ground cinnamon, cardamom, cloves, nutmeg and black pepper

1¼ cups mixed dried fruits

½ cup blanched almonds

½ cup pine nuts

½ cup shelled hazelnuts, toasted

3-4 tbsp all-purpose flour, sifted

4 tbsp Vin Santo

Confectioner's sugar for dusting

Serves 10

1 Heat the oven to 300° F. Line a shallow 10-inch round cake pan with rice paper.

2 Place the chopped figs or dates, or a mix of the two, in a pot with just enough water to cover. Add the honey, brown sugar and all the spices. Cook gently for about 10 minutes, then tip into a bowl. The mixture should be soft and sticky but not wet.

3 Add the mixed fruits and all the nuts and mix well, then add the flour and Vin Santo and mix to a sticky mass. Spoon the mixture into the prepared pan and bake in the oven for 30–40 minutes.

4 Remove the panforte from the oven and leave to cool in the pan. Sprinkle generously with the confectioner's sugar, then cut into wedges and serve.

WALNUT

Botanical name: *Juglans regia*
Family: *Juglandaceae*

A walnut is the nut of any tree of the genus *Juglans* (Family *Juglandaceae*), particularly the Persian or English walnut, *Juglans regia*. The walnut tree is thought to have originated in central Asia. The walnut is not the fruit of the walnut tree but the seed within the fruit. They are ready for harvesting in the late summer, when their thick green hulls begin to crack open to expose the light- brown, hard-shelled 'walnut' inside.

Walnuts are grown commercially in the United States, Romania, France, Turkey and China, and are available throughout the year from all grocery stores and markets. They

can be bought whole or shelled in their natural form or can be processed with salt or sugar. The kernels have a nutty yet pleasantly sweet flavor and can be used for a variety of culinary purposes. They are particularly good in salads, desserts containing fruits, and in ice creams and cakes. They can also be used in yogurts and pizzas and go particularly well with blue cheese. In the Middle East they are often combined with dishes containing raisins. When buying walnuts, look for nuts that are bright in color and free from mold or cracks. Ensure that there is no rancid smell.

Health benefits: Walnuts are beneficial to health in a number of ways: they contain omega-3 essential fatty acids, which are good for cardiovascular health, and they have abundant monounsaturated and polyunsaturated fats which benefit the heart and offer protection against high blood pressure, stroke and high (bad) cholesterol levels. Walnuts also help to prevent diabetes, enhance the skin, being rich in vitamin E, and are high in antioxidants. They are also a good source of melatonin, which is a treatment for insomnia.

CHICORY BOATS WITH BLUE CHEESE, PEAR & WALNUTS

16 Belgian chicory leaves
1½ oz Gorgonzola cheese, crumbled
1 oz walnuts, toasted and roughly chopped
2 tsp finely chopped parsley, plus some for a garnish
2 tbsp balsamic vinegar

Serves 2

1 Arrange 8 chicory leaves on each of two serving plates.

2 Mix the Gorgonzola, nuts and parsley together in a small bowl.

3 Spoon a little of the mixture into each leaf.

4. Drizzle with balsamic vinegar, then garnish with parsley and serve.

PASTA WITH WALNUT SAUCE

12 oz rigatoni
2 tbsp olive oil
½ cup walnuts (for the sauce)
2 tbsp milk
3 tbsp sour cream
½ cup grated Parmesan cheese
3 cloves garlic, minced
Salt and pepper to taste
¼ cup roughly chopped walnuts to garnish
¼ cup chopped chives

Serves 4

1 Cook the pasta according to the package directions. Lightly toast the walnuts (for the sauce) in a dry skillet, making sure they do not burn.

2 In a blender, process the toasted walnuts to the texture of coarse breadcrumbs.

3 To a medium-sized pot, add the milk, sour cream, Parmesan cheese, garlic, blended walnuts, salt and pepper, stirring until the sauce thickens.

4 Divide the pasta between serving bowls and top with the sauce.

5 Sprinkle over the garnish of roughly chopped walnuts and chopped chives and serve.

PISTACHIO

Botanical name: *Pistacia vera*
Family: *Anacardiaceae*

The pistachio, a close relative of the cashew, is a small shrubby tree native to central Asia and the Middle East, where it has flourished for centuries. Although commonly regarded as a nut, the fruit is in fact a drupe containing an elongated seed, which is the edible portion. The pistachio is also one of the oldest of the flowering 'nut' trees, with recent archeological evidence suggesting that it existed in Turkey at least 7,000 years ago.

There is a well-known legend that the Queen of Sheba decreed pistachios an exclusively royal food, and commoners were forbidden to cultivate them, while Nebuchadnezzar, the ancient

king of Babylon is said to have planted pistachios in his fabled hanging gardens.

Today, while Middle Eastern countries are the main producers of pistachios, they are also grown in the United States, particularly in California, where the climate is suitably mild. Pistachios were originally imported into California in the

1880s as garden trees, but many years of careful cultivation have produced a successful variety capable of producing a high yield of nuts. Today, California is the second largest producer of pistachios in the world after Iran.

Pistachios are used in a variety of culinary ways, famously in Italian ice creams and in the Middle Eastern *baklava*, a sweet pastry made from layers of filo filled with chopped nuts and honey. Roasted pistachios are often shelled and sprinkled over salads and desserts, when their beautiful green colour becomes immediately apparent.

Health benefits: Pistachios are a rich source of many phyto-chemical substances that may contribute to their overall antioxidant activity, including carotenes, vitamin E and polyphenolic antioxidant compounds. Research studies have suggested that these compounds help remove toxic oxygen-free radicals from the body, and thus protect it from diseases such as cancers as well as common infections.

PISTACHIO ICE CREAM

1 cup toasted, unsalted pistachios,
 shells removed
1 cup sugar
1 cup whole milk
1 tsp almond extract
3 large eggs
A few drops green food
 coloring
2 cups heavy cream
An additional ¾ cup chopped
 pistachios

1 In a food processor, blend the
cupful of pistachios with ½ cup of
the sugar.

2 Put the milk into a pot and add
the pistachio mixture. Bring the
mixture to a boil and, as it starts to
boil, remove it from the heat and
add the almond extract.

3 In a medium-sized bowl, whisk
the eggs. Add the remaining sugar
and continue to whisk until the
sugar is incorporated. Mix in a
few drops of the food coloring, a
drop at a time, until the desired
effect is achieved.

4 Slowly incorporate the hot milk
and pistachio mixture into the egg

mixture. Return the mixture to the
pot and turn the heat on to low.
Allow the mixture to simmer for
10 minutes, but do not let it boil.

5 Pour the mixture back into the
bowl and leave it in the
refrigerator until thoroughly
chilled (approximately 2 hours).

6 Stir in the heavy cream and the
remaining pistachios, then pour
the entire mixture into an ice
cream maker. Follow the
manufacturer's instructions to
process.

7 Sprinkle the finished ice cream
with a little grated chocolate and
mint leaves.

NOTE: Pistachio ice cream made
without artificial coloring is
usually a creamy color with only a
hint of green.

ALMOND

Botanical name: *Prunus dulcis*
Family: *Rosaceae*

The almond is a deciduous tree, native to the Middle East and South Asia, which is cultivated for its nuts. Contrary to what most people think, however, the fruit of the almond is a drupe rather than a nut, and consists of an outer hull and hard shell with the seed inside.

The almond tree is related to the peach, cherry and apricot. Almonds come in two categories: sweet (*Prunus amygdalu var. dulcis*) and bitter (*Prunus amygdalu var. amara*). Sweet almonds are the type that are eaten as they are, with the bitter type going for oil and the alcholic drink, amaretto.

Bitter almonds are toxic unless they have been processed to have the toxins removed.

The wild form of almond, that grows throughout the Levant, contains glycoside amygdalin which, once handled or ingested, becomes transformed into deadly hydrogen cyanide after crushing, chewing, or any other injury to the seed. Even eating a few dozen nuts at one time can be fatal. While the wild almond is poisonous the cultivated one is not, for it has been bred so that the amygdalin content is removed. Commercially grown almonds are selected so that no bitter toxins are present in any wild or bitter varieties.

Almonds may be eaten raw or toasted and can also be flaked or slivered. Almonds yield almond oil and can also be made into butter or almond milk, which is becoming increasingly more popular. The delicately flavored almond is readily available and can be added to breakfast cereals and desserts; it is famously used in curries, marzipan, nougat, amaretti and macaroons.

Health benefits: Almonds are packed with great nutrients, their fats being mostly mono-unsaturated (the type associated with olive oil). They are an excellent source of vitamin E and manganese, and a good or very good source of many other vitamins and minerals, including magnesium. Almonds also contain large amounts of phytonutrients, especially plant sterols and flavonoids, which are good for the heart, as well as helpful antioxidants. Enjoy your almonds with the inner skins left on, rather than blanched, which is where the flavonoids are concentrated.

CINNAMON-ROASTED ALMONDS & PECANS

1 large egg white
1 tsp cold water
1 cup shelled almonds
1 cup shelled pecans
½ cup brown sugar
½ tsp ground cinnamon
¼ tsp salt

1 Preheat the oven to 250°F. Lightly oil a large sheet pan.

2 In a large bowl, lightly beat the egg white, add the water, then beat together until light and frothy. Add the nuts, and stir until well-coated. Mix the sugar, cinnamon and salt together in a separate bowl, then add the nuts, tossing them about until well-coated. Spread the nuts out evenly on the prepared sheet pan.

3 Bake for 1 hour until golden, shaking the nuts occasionally to ensure they are all thoroughly roasted. Allow to cool before serving.

ALMOND & COCONUT MACAROONS

3 large egg whites
¾ tsp almond extract
½ cup sugar
¼ tsp salt
1¾ cups flaked, sweetened coconut

1 Preheat the oven to 325ºF. Line a sheet pan with baking parchment.

2 In a large bowl, whisk together the egg whites, almond extract, sugar and salt until light and frothy. Add the coconut and mix well together.

3 Shape the mixture into small mounds, using your hands (about 2 tablespoonfuls per macaroon). Place each macaroon on the sheet pan at about ½ an inch apart.

4 Bake for 30–40 minutes until lightly golden in color, turning the sheet pan around halfway through the cooking time. Transfer the macaroons to a wire rack to cool completely.

All images in this book, including the
cover are supplied by: ©
Shutterstock.com